Published in 1988 by
The Hamlyn Publishing Group Limited
Michelin House, 81 Fulham Road,
London SW3 6RB

ISBN 0 600 55584 4

Printed in Italy

Typeset in Monophoto Bembo by
Vision Typesetting, Manchester

the SPINE CHILLING book of MONSTERS

Rupert Matthews

Consultant Francis X. King

HAMLYN

CONTENTS

Introduction

Monsters have haunted mankind from his earliest days. Cavemen painted fantastic creatures on the rocky walls of their homes and the poets and storytellers of ancient times recited tales of hideous beasts which could only be overcome by mighty heroes.

Even in modern times, the monster continues to dominate our imaginations. Films such as *The Creature from the Black Lagoon* and *Jaws* fill cinema screens with monstrous animals dedicated to destruction. As in the old tales, only a hero can overcome these new monsters.

But not all monsters are fictitious. Hundreds of people claim to have sighted a monster speeding across Loch Ness and many more have seen a similar beast in the open sea. The mountains of the Himalayas and British Columbia are said to be the home of large man-apes, which still elude scientific description.

Monsters are all around us. In books, films, our imaginations and real life, monsters continue to lurk, waiting to pounce. It is a brave person who does not secretly fear the beasts within this book.

WATER MONSTERS

Sea Serpents

For centuries sailors and fishermen have been saying that there is a very strange and extremely large monster living in the ocean. Hundreds of people claim to have seen the sea serpent, as it is called. The descriptions given of this monster vary in detail, but all agree that the beast is extremely large. Despite these well-authenticated reports, the animal remains completely unknown to science.

Many early sightings of giant sea creatures were made by simple men who could neither read nor write. These men did not record their stories so we know little about the creatures which they claim to have seen. Possibly the earliest reliable report of a sea monster is that made by Hans Egede, a distinguished clergyman, in about 1734.

In that year Hans Egede was sailing to Greenland. As his ship drew close to the coast a huge, snake-like animal reared out of the water nearby. Egede says that "its head reached as high as the masthead; its body was as bulky as the ship, and three or four times as long." Judging by the size of Egede's ship, the animal was about 40 metres (130 feet) in length.

Twelve years later Lorenz von Ferry, the commander of a Norwegian ship, sighted a similar animal in the North Sea. At the time of his sighting von Ferry was being rowed ashore by men from his ship. Some distance away what appeared to be a huge creature broke the surface.

A 19th-century engraving of a sea monster based upon sailors' tales.

Showing much courage, von Ferry ordered the men to row close to the animal. Von Ferry thought the creature was about 18 metres (60 feet) long and had a mane around its neck. The strange animal swam off after von Ferry fired a shotgun at it.

Interesting as these reports are, they provide little detail of the animal which was alleged to have been seen. Very different are the reports of the sea serpent which seems to have found its way into a large bay known as Gloucester Harbour on the Atlantic coast of Massachusetts.

This strange creature was first sighted on 10 August 1817 by a man named Amos Story. According to his evidence, Amos was "setting on the shore and was about 20 rods (100 metres) from him". At this distance it is unlikely that an

Many reports speak of sea serpents having long, sharp teeth.

experienced fisherman would be mistaken in what he saw. Story reported "His head appeared shaped much like the head of the sea-turtle, and from ten to 12 inches (25 to 30 centimetres) above the surface of the water. I did not see more than ten or 12 feet (three or four metres) of his body."

Over the following two weeks dozens of local fishermen and townsfolk saw the serpent. Greatly excited, the Linnaean Society of Boston, a prominent naturalist organization, sent a committee to Gloucester to collect evidence. The committee persuaded many witnesses to make statements describing what they had seen. Because of this evidence, the Gloucester sea serpent is one of the best recorded of such creatures.

The descriptions of the monster contained in the committee's report are colourful, but consistent. Solomen Allen stated "I should judge him to be between 80 and 90 feet (26 to 28 metres), and about the size of a half barrel apparently heavy jointed from his head to tail."

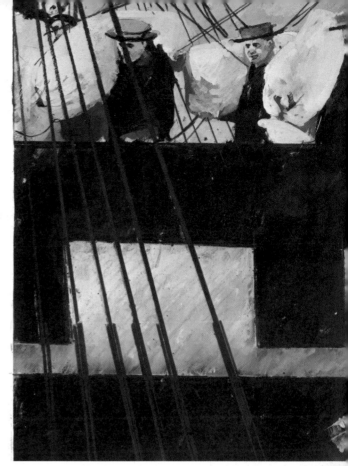

This 19th-century engraving is entitled The Sea Serpent in Gloucester Harbour. *Though rather fanciful, the artist clearly followed eye-witness accounts of the monster.*

When the sailors stepped ashore, they found the whole town eager for news of the monster.

ship docked, the crew were unsure whether or not to mention their frightening encounter. They did not want to be thought of as credulous idiots by those who would not believe their story. However, the men need not have worried. As soon as they stepped on shore a large crowd pressed forward to ask if the sailors had seen the serpent.

The many eye-witness reports of the creature seen at Gloucester seem to agree. The beast was about 35 metres (125 feet) long and some two metres (six feet) in circumference. The creature appeared to be a giant snake, with a reptilian head and smooth skin. Nobody had the slightest idea what this creature was, and to this day no adequate explanation has been put forward.

On 12 December 1965 a very similar creature to that reported by the people of Gloucester was seen at close quarters off the Australian east

Sewall Toppan thought that "the head appeared to be the size of a ten-gallon (45-litre) keg". William Pearson was vaguer. He merely said he had sighted "a strange marine animal of great size".

Some days after the serpent was first sighted, a whaling ship put into Gloucester. As the ship approached shore the monster rose up out of the sea just 200 metres (220 yards) away. The sailors were badly frightened by the huge animal, which seemed to be following the ship. They were greatly relieved when the unwelcome visitor suddenly dived from view. When the coast. The mystery beast was even photographed. The creature was discovered by Robert le Serrec, a Frenchman, and an Australian named Henk de Jong. According to their story, they came across it in the shallow waters of the Great Barrier Reef. The creature was some 20 metres (65 feet) long and had a large head. About halfway along the body was a long, gaping wound. The creature appeared to be dead.

After taking photographs of the creature from the surface, le Serrec and de Jong put on diving gear and slipped into the water. As the two men approached with their cameras the serpent moved. It was very much alive. "The mouth opened menacingly several times", recalled le Serrac. "We swam frantically towards the boat." As the men scrambled to safety, the animal swam off into deep water and disappeared from sight.

These reports, and many others, indicate that a gigantic snake-like animal is living in the ocean. However, other reports are very different. They seem to suggest that there is another type of monster prowling the open sea. In fact this type of mystery monster, with a long neck, small head and large body, is that most often reported by seamen. Literally hundreds of sightings of this large creature are on record.

Perhaps the earliest and best documented sighting of this beast occurred in 1848 in the South Atlantic. On 6 August at 5 pm, seven officers and men of HMS *Daedalus* spotted a huge animal approaching their corvette. The creature was in sight for a quarter of an hour and, according to Captain M'Quhae, came "so close under our lee quarter, that had it been a man of my acquaintance I should have easily recognized his features". It seems unlikely that a captain in the Royal Navy should mistake what he saw at such a distance and almost unthinkable that he and his crew would invent the story.

The creature described by Captain M'Quhae was at least 20 metres (65 feet) long. It had a rounded head which it held slightly above the water. The neck was some 40 centimetres (two feet) in diameter and was darker on top than underneath. M'Quhae reported that the creature swam on a straight course at a speed of some

12 knots, which is fast for an animal of such a size. Although it moved quickly, the witnesses noticed that the body did not undulate as that of a swimming snake would. This suggests that the creature had flippers which remained under the water.

The possibility of flippers on this type of sea monster seems to be confirmed by a sighting in the Orkneys in 1919. A group of lobster fishermen were startled when a long neck and small head suddenly rose out of the water close to their boat. As the men watched in alarm, the head sank below the water and the creature swam beneath the boat. The creature was said to be about seven metres (23 feet) long and swam by means of four paddles which it flapped through the water.

Far larger was the monster sighted by the officers of SS *Tyne* in 1920. The length of this beast was estimated at 28 metres (93 feet), the neck alone measuring ten metres (33 feet). According to the report, the strange creature swam alongside the ship for some time and seemed to be inspecting the vessel.

In most reports, the sea monster is said to be alarming, but does no damage to either ships or men. In contrast, the creature which is said to have appeared near Florida in 1962 was terrifying in the extreme. On 24th March of that year five skin-diving enthusiasts put out to sea on a raft to investigate a submerged wreck. After some time a fog came down. As the men sat on their raft, they heard strange splashing noises made by a large animal approaching. Worried that they might be capsized, the men put on their diving gear and took to the water.

As they were swimming in the water, the men sighted a long neck, topped by a large head approaching them. Suddenly, the monster dashed forwards. One of the divers screamed in agony and disappeared. Soon afterwards, the monster returned. Another man screamed and vanished. Only one member of the party survived this terrifying encounter with a predator from the deep. It is not known if the monster actually ate the missing men, but in the circumstances this would seem the likely, if awful, conclusion.

A smaller mystery creature was seen by two

The coelacanth, once thought extinct, is now known to live off the coast of South Africa. Main picture: a photograph of le Serrec's monster.

A scene from the film The Beast from 20,000 Fathoms.

professional zoologists in the South Atlantic in 1905. The professional status of these men makes their story more believable. The men were part of a scientific expedition on board the yacht *Valhalla* at the time and made careful note of what they had seen. Upon their return to London the two men presented a report to the Zoological Society of London. The society was interested but refused to believe in the accuracy of the alleged sighting.

This seems to be typical of the reaction of scientific institutions to the question of the sea serpent. They do not wish to accept the existence of such a fabulous monster without firm evidence. They prefer either to discount the reports or simply to ignore them.

According to scientific principles, no animal can be accepted as genuine unless scientists have an actual example to study. It does not matter whether the specimen is alive or dead, so long as it is in front of them. Eye-witness reports, no matter how reliable, are not accepted as evidence for the real existence of a monster.

Scientists point out that there is always the possibility that the witness was mistaken in what was seen. Scientists often try to discount reports of sea monsters by suggesting that the witness actually saw something else. For instance Richard Owen, a noted naturalist of the time, suggested that Captain M'Quhae had seen nothing more unusual than a large seal. Captain M'Quhae angrily denied this suggestion. One authority tried to explain away the creature sighted from the *Valhalla* as a swordfish with a smaller fish impaled on its sword.

The long-running arguments about the sea monster were nearly settled in April 1977. Fishing the waters of the southern Pacific, the Japanese trawler *Zuiyo Maru* hauled a strange creature up in its nets. The animal had been dead for some time and was partially decomposed. The creature appeared to have a small head on a long neck and four flippers. Captain Tanaka, who commanded the ship, thought that he had caught a sea monster.

Captain Tanaka at first intended to bring the carcass to port for study. Unfortunately, the body began to rot with such speed that it became a health hazard and threatened to infect all the fish on board the *Zuiyo Maru*. Captain Tanaka hurriedly photographed, measured and drew the beast and then dumped it overboard. When scientists looked at the evidence they declared that the body had probably been that of a shark.

Despite these official statements, the question

is far from settled. Although no sea serpent has been caught and subjected to scientific study this does not mean that no such creature exists. Until 1976 no scientist suspected that the megamouth shark existed. But a ship of the United States Navy found a specimen of this creature entangled with its anchor. The megamouth weighs nearly a ton and is a fearsome predator.

If the megamouth shark can survive without anybody catching or even seeing one, it is possible that the sea serpent may indeed exist. There is plenty of room in the ocean for such a monster to live and more than enough food for it to eat. Perhaps one day, somebody will catch a sea serpent and we shall know exactly what type of animal it really is.

The Loch Ness Monster

There is said to be a huge, unknown monster lurking in the depths of Loch Ness, a lake in northern Scotland. Loch Ness is about 40 kilometres (24 miles) long and 1.5 kilometres (one mile) wide. It is thought to be about 230 metres (750 feet) deep. Dozens of people have claimed to have seen the fearsome beast, sometimes at very close quarters, and many people have taken photographs of what appears to be the creature. It is difficult to believe that all these reports are hoaxes or mistakes. On the other hand, no firm evidence for the existence of the monster has ever been produced.

The controversy surrounding Loch Ness began in 1933, on 2 May to be precise. On that day the *Inverness Courier*, a local newspaper, printed a sensational report. Under the heading "Strange Spectacle in Loch Ness", the paper described the experiences of John and Donaldina Mackay. They had been driving on the newly constructed road along the northern shore of Loch Ness when Mrs Mackay noticed a disturbance in the water. She could not see exactly what was causing the water to froth, but guessed that it was an animal many feet in length.

The newspaper article reporting the event was picked up by national newspapers and soon the Loch Ness monster became known to people all over the world. In fact, the Mackay report was not the first sighting of the monster on record. Several earlier reports of a large animal had been made, but they had not become well known outside the district.

A Monster in Parliament

On 12 November 1933, the subject of the Loch Ness monster was raised in the British Parliament. A member of Parliament asked the government to set up an inquiry to discover if the monster really existed or not. The request was turned down. The government felt that it had better things to spend its money on.

The idea of a monster in Loch Ness was obscured by local folklore. Many highland Scots believed in the existence of a supernatural beast known as a kelpie. This creature was thought to live in lochs and was said to be very fierce. In the early years of this century, the kelpie was treated

Despite several close encounters with the alleged monster of Loch Ness, its existence has not yet been proved.

A famous 1934 photograph of the monster with Alex Campbell (left) and Evan Barron (right).

as something of a joke. Anybody who reported such an animal would be open to ridicule. It is possible that many people kept quiet about the monster in order to avoid such mockery. Early reports of the Loch Ness monster referred to it as a kelpie. Similar beliefs were held in Ireland and water monsters have been reported here in recent years. Lough Fadda, Lough Dubh and Lough Brin are all said to be the home of monsters.

Interest in the Loch Ness monster boomed when photographs of the beast were taken. In November 1933 Hugh Gray produced an indistinct picture of a serpent-like creature. Five months later R. K. Wilson photographed what seems to be a tall neck with a small head perched on top of it. This picture convinced many people that the monster existed, but many others remained sceptical.

Over the following years, many other people claimed to have seen the monster. Some of the witnesses had cameras with them and were able to take snapshots of what they saw. On 21 May 1977, Anthony Shiels took a particularly fine photograph. The colour shot appears to show a dark neck projecting from the loch. On top of the neck can be seen a small head with partially opened jaws.

On 23 April 1960, Tim Dinsdale thought that he saw the monster swimming across the loch and filmed it. His movie shows a large object moving rapidly through the water. The film has been subjected to study by photographic experts and has been pronounced to be genuine.

These chance sightings of the monster encouraged many people to travel to Loch Ness with the intention of proving that the monster really does exist. In 1970, the American scientist Doctor Robert Rines and a team of helpers arrived equipped with sonar, underwater cameras and a host of other equipment.

Over the following years, Dr Rines produced some very interesting evidence. The sonar, used by naval vessels to track submarines, revealed several large moving objects in the loch. Unfortunately, it was not clear what these objects were. The cameras produced more interesting results. Despite the dark, peaty waters, a few good photographs were produced. The most

The Champion Monster Spotter

Most witnesses who see the Loch Ness monster only see it once and for a short time. However, Alex Campbell claims to have seen the monster no less than 18 times. He works as the water bailiff of Loch Ness, so his job takes him out onto the water far more often than most people. This means that he is in a good position to witness any unusual sight on the lake.

famous of these showed a large, diamond-shaped flipper and part of a body. Another photograph seemed to show a long neck and small head.

The photograph of Nessie by Hugh Gray (right)

A diver working for the BBC, after his unsuccessful attempt to find the monster.

The Saint and the Monster

Fourteen centuries ago the holy man, St Columba, was travelling through the Scottish Highlands preaching the gospel and converting pagans. When he reached the banks of the River Ness, which flows out of Loch Ness, he came across a fearsome monster. A man was swimming in the river when the monster appeared and swam quickly towards him with jaws open. St Columba commanded the monster to leave the man alone, whereupon it dived from sight.

In October 1987 the £1 million Operation Deepscan led by Adrian Shine was launched. A line of boats carrying sonar equipment cruised slowly along Loch Ness. Nearly the entire loch was searched for the monster. The results of the operation were inconclusive. Several large objects were located, but it was not clear what they were.

The accumulated evidence of scientific equipment and of eye-witnesses can be used to put together a picture of the alleged monster. The elusive being would seem to be quite large, perhaps as a long as ten metres (33 feet), and it has a long neck and a small head. The animal might be propelled through the water by four flippers attached to its body. It seems most likely that the animal, if it exists, feeds on fish.

No scientist has been able to suggest to which type of animal this description might apply. Some people think that the monster is a type of prehistoric reptile known as a plesiosaur. Though this creature looked very much like the Loch Ness monster, it has been extinct for 65 million years. Other theories suggest that the monster is a type of fish, mammal or even mollusc. However, serious objections can be brought against each suggestion.

Despite the evidence of sonar and cameras, controversy about the monster has continued to rage. Evidence continues to be produced, but nothing definite has yet been found. It seems almost unbelievable that a large animal could live in a British lake without being well-known to science. In fact, some people doubt that a large animal can survive in Loch Ness at all. They point out that the loch is quite a small body of water. This raises certain problems with the monster theory.

If there is a Loch Ness monster, more than one must exist. For any type of animal to survive for any length of time, there needs to be a breeding population. This might mean that about 20 monsters would need to live in Loch Ness at any one time. Sceptics state that if there were 20 large animals in the loch, they should be seen far more often than is the case. Others say that the fact that the monsters are rarely seen simply indicates that they do not often come to the surface of the loch.

The monsters would also need enough food to sustain themselves. A recent study by two Canadian scientists was carried out to discover if there was enough food in Loch Ness for the monsters. They found that the loch was rich in fish, with species such as eels, pike and salmon.

The studies showed that there are enough fish in Loch Ness to provide food for a breeding population of monsters around eight metres (25 feet) long. This does not, however, prove that the monsters do exist.

One of the points raised by sceptics is the fact that no dead monster has ever been found. If a population of monsters lives in Loch Ness, a specimen must die from time to time. Dead bodies usually float, so when a monster dies its body should be washed ashore. The fact that this has not happened is strong evidence against the Loch Ness monster. However, the loch is very deep and may swallow up any dead monsters. It is also possible that the monsters migrate into the sea from the lake, so their bodies would not be left in the loch at all.

The whole problem of Loch Ness can be summed up by a single sighting. In July 1933 Mr and Mrs Spicer were motoring along the side of the lake. It was 4 o'clock on a bright sunny day. Suddenly they saw a large animal lumber across the road just 50 metres (55 yards) in front of them and dive into the loch. Mr Spicer later described the creature as "very ugly".

The fact that Mr Spicer says that he saw the monster at such short range makes it unlikely, but not impossible, that he was mistaken in what he saw. However, some people have suggested that Mr Spicer invented the story, perhaps to get his name in the newspapers. If, however, the story is to be believed there can be little doubt that the Loch Ness monster is a reality.

The Monster and Royalty

During the 19th century Queen Victoria and Prince Albert came to Loch Ness on one of their many visits to the Highlands of Scotland. Unfortunately for those who believe in the monster, the royal couple reported nothing at all unusual in the loch.

Queen Victoria's great grand-daughter, on the other hand, knew about the monster from a very early age. When just three years old Princess Margaret was shown a picture of a dragon. "What a darling little Loch Ness monster," she exclaimed.

In recent years, scientists, such as those from the Academy of Applied Science in the USA (above), have investigated Loch Ness with sophisticated equipment. They produced the slightly blurred underwater photograph (below right) which many claim shows the monster's head, neck and part of its body. The exceptionally clear picture (below left) was taken by Anthony Shiels.

In Asian Lakes

Tales of large monsters are not restricted to lakes in the Gaelic countries of Scotland and Ireland, where tales of supernatural kelpies abound. As recently as 1980 news came from China that similar monsters were to be found in that Far Eastern country.

In September of that year sightings of large animals in the Tian Chi Lake were made. The creatures were said to be about the size of a cow and to have a head with a duck's beak. Perhaps the most interesting feature of this report is that Tian Chi is a flooded volcanic crater formed by an eruption in 1702. If the monsters exist, they cannot be indigenous to the lake. They must have moved overland from another lake.

One of the people who saw the Tian Chi monster said that he watched a group of five monsters for some time. This seems to indicate that there is a breeding population of beasts in the lake, which is a point in favour of their existence. In August 1980, a local man sighted what he thought was the monster. The man had his gun with him, so he shot at the monster and later claimed to have wounded it. However, as he did not catch the beast, this is again inconclusive.

Far more dramatic is the huge beast which terrorizes the lands around Wenbu Lake. Situated high on the Tibetan plateau, this lake

Lake monsters in Asia seem to be particularly aggressive. They have been blamed for the disappearance of cattle and men as well as other, smaller animals.

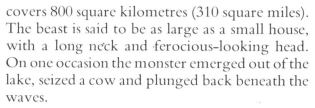

covers 800 square kilometres (310 square miles). The beast is said to be as large as a small house, with a long neck and ferocious-looking head. On one occasion the monster emerged out of the lake, seized a cow and plunged back beneath the waves.

Some locals blamed the monster for the death of a man who was drowned when rowing across the lake. His small boat suddenly overturned for no apparent reason and the man was dragged down in a great disturbance of water.

In 1981, scientists visited the lake and investigated the reports. Though they did not return with any conclusive evidence, the scientists reported that the people who lived near the lake certainly believed that such a beast existed. Even local government officials had seen the animal.

During the 1950s, other monsters were sighted in Asian lakes when a team of Russian scientists were exploring the vast and uninhabited Dimyakon tableland in Siberia. Two members of the expedition were working on the shores of Lake Vorota when a movement in the water caught their attention. They looked up to see a huge animal about ten metres (33 feet) long splashing about on the surface.

Ten years later another expedition was visiting the nearby Lake Khaiyr. The scientists were told by the native hunters of the region that Lake Khaiyr contained a large animal which it was best to avoid. Taking no notice of such tales, one scientist strolled down to the lake one morning and came face to face with a creature he had never seen before.

Emerging from the forest, the man suddenly saw the monster sitting on the lake shore right in front of him. It had a large body, topped by an upright fin, and a long neck with a small head. The man turned round and fled as fast as he could. When he returned with other members of the party, the beast had gone. It was, however, seen a few days later by other scientists in the group.

A model of Ogopogo which can be found at Kelowna on the shores of Lake Okanagan.

In American Lakes

The Indians of North America were firm believers in lake monsters. They believed that huge creatures lived in many of the lakes scattered across Canada and the northern states of the USA. When European settlers began to occupy the continent, the Indians warned them about the monsters. About 150 years ago, trouble flared up between settlers and the Potawatomi tribe of Indiana. The settlers had built a water mill which the Indians said would disturb the local lake monster.

At first such tales were discounted by white settlers. However, some of the newcomers quickly changed their minds when they thought they saw the monsters themselves. Bear Lake in Utah was the site of many monster sightings during the 19th century, as was Elkhart Lake in Wisconsin.

More recent sightings of strange monsters occur most often in Canada. The most famous of all Canadian lake monsters has been nick-named Ogopogo and is said to live in Lake Okanagan, a 130-kilometre (80-mile) long body of water in British Columbia.

The earliest reports of a monster in this lake date back to the middle of the last century, but the most reliable sightings have occurred in more recent years. In July 1952, Mrs Campbell of Vancouver paid a visit to a friend whose house stands on the lake shore. Suddenly, the women saw a huge animal come into sight less than 100 metres (330 feet) away. According to the report, the upright neck of the animal appeared first, carrying a "head like a horse". Then a series of glistening humps rose above the water behind the neck. After remaining on the surface for some time, the creature dived from sight.

Seven years after Mrs Campbell claimed to sight Ogopogo, Dick Miller, a newspaper editor, was travelling across Lake Okanagan in a motor cruiser. Suddenly he saw an object following his craft about 75 metres (250 feet) away. Using his binoculars, Miller focused on his mystery pursuer. He saw a head standing some 25 centimetres (nine inches) out of the water followed by five humps. Miller started to

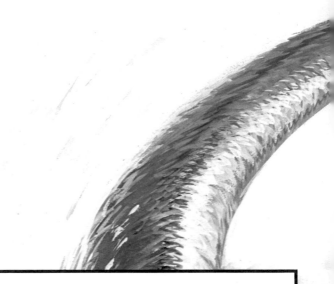

Part of the team which spent many days hunting for the monster of Lake Champlain.

approach the strange being, but it dived from sight. More recently two locals reported seeing the monster racing along the lake at high speed.

Dozens of people claim to have seen Ogopogo and most of these reports agree with each other. The beast is said to be about 20 metres (66 feet) long and shaped like a snake with a large head. Its colour is usually described as dark green. Ogopogo has become a tourist attraction in the area. Even the Department of Recreation and Conservation of the provincial government has erected signs around the lake giving the story of Ogopogo.

Lake Champlain, which straddles the border between Canada and the USA, is claimed to be the home of a very similar monster to that in Lake Okanagan. Settlers of the early 19th century believed that a large animal lived in the lake and several people reported catching a glimpse of it. Reports of a mystery monster in

The motives of lake monsters have been open to various interpretations over the centuries. According to many traditional beliefs, the creatures are said to be evil and powerful. The Dutch pilot whose helicopter had a narrow escape from a monster thought he was being attacked. However, the huge creature may simply have been curious.

the water have continued to be made down to the present day. In 1977 a photograph of the animal appeared, but sceptics thought that the picture showed a perfectly normal animal from an odd angle.

Even Africa has its tales of water monsters. Flying low over a lake in Africa, a Dutch helicopter pilot received the shock of his life. A long neck carrying a huge head suddenly emerged from the lake and struck at his aircraft. Swerving to one side, the pilot fled at high speed.

GIANT REPTILES

Dinosaurs, Ancient and Modern

Perhaps the greatest monsters which have ever existed were the dinosaurs. These huge reptiles lived many millions of years ago. Some species were probably the largest animals ever to have lived, while others were smaller than a chicken.

Although these creatures were both large and common, man has only recently become aware that they ever existed. About 200 years ago nobody suspected that such creatures had once stalked the Earth. Then scientists began finding large fossilized bones in ancient rock strata. The bones clearly belonged to reptiles, but they were much larger than any species living today.

Nobody was sure what to make of the new discoveries. But in 1841 the famous British scientist, Richard Owen, suggested that the creatures whose fossils had been found might belong to a completely different group of reptiles. He called them dinosaurs, which is Greek for "terrible reptile".

In the years which followed Owen's suggestion many more fossils were found. Today's scientists are able to reconstruct different dinosaurs with a fair degree of accuracy. The size, appearance and probable lifestyle of many dinosaurs can be deduced from the fossil evidence.

By studying fossils, scientists know that the first dinosaurs were quite small, perhaps just over a metre (four feet) long, and ran on their hind legs. They evolved rapidly to produce a wide variety of strange and wonderful creatures. Within a few million years there were plant-eating dinosaurs, armoured dinosaurs, large meat-eaters and small, nimble hunters.

Some of the most dramatic of all dinosaurs were those which evolved last. One of these was the mighty *Tyrannosaurus rex* which lived about 70 million years ago in North America. This fearsome meat-eating dinosaur measured about 12 metres (39 feet) in length and reached 5.5 metres (18 feet) tall. The jaws of *Tyrannosaurus* were armed with dozens of teeth each 18 centimetres (seven inches) long. These fangs were extremely sharp and serrated like steak knives, which made them highly efficient at tearing lumps of meat from prey. The power and ferocity of *Tyrannosaurus rex* fully lived up to the creature's name, which means "King of the Tyrant Reptiles".

Living at the same time as *Tyrannosaurus* was one of the most famous of all dinosaurs, *Trice-*

The term "dinosaur" was first used by Sir Richard Owen, a British scientist.

The mighty meat-eater Tyrannosaurus rex *confronts the plant-eater* Triceratops.

ratops. This creature had three large, sharp horns growing out of its head, these gave the monster its name which means "three-horned face". There can be little doubt that if *Triceratops* were attacked by a hunter, it would lower its head and charge. The dangerous horns would be enough to deter almost any predator.

Triceratops was only one of many horned dinosaurs. *Styracosaurus* was smaller, but was one of the most terrifying. Like *Triceratops*, it had a large bone frill which projected from the back of the skull, but on the frill there were sharp spikes which projected backwards like a line of horns.

If these creatures relied upon their horns for defence, another group of dinosaurs evolved tough bony armour for the same purpose. First appearing about 110 million years ago, the ankylosaurs never became numerous, but they survived for nearly 50 million years. Possibly the largest ankylosaur was also the last. *Ankylosaurus* was over ten metres (35 feet) long, which means that it was larger than many modern battle tanks and had armour almost as effective. It could also strike back with a heavy club of bone at the end of its tail.

Relying on a very different system of defence were the smaller plant-eating dinosaurs such as *Hypsilophodon*. These creatures relied upon their ability to run quickly to escape from danger. The fossils of these animals show them to have been both nimble and speedy. Of several dozen similar dinosaur species, few were more than three metres (ten feet) long.

Even faster than the small plant-eaters were the creatures known as ostrich dinosaurs. Some of these creatures could have run faster than a

galloping horse. However, scientists have little idea how these animals lived. They had no teeth at all, so they could have eaten neither meat nor vegetation. Some think that these odd creatures may have eaten insects or fruit, but nobody is very sure.

A powerful killer was *Deinonychus*, whose name means "Terrible Claw". This dinosaur was about the size of a man, but was far stronger. Each of its muscular hind legs was armed with a curved claw some 12 centimetres (five inches) long. *Deinonychus* could run fast enough to catch most other types of dinosaur. Using its strong claw, this fearsome hunter could rip up and kill any creature it could catch.

The most spectacular dinosaurs of all, however, were the huge plant-eaters known as sauropods. These massive creatures weighed many tons and roamed around the countryside in large herds. They had long necks with small heads perched on top, and long thin tails. Some scientists think that sauropods lived in swamps and ate soft water plants. Other specialists believe that sauropods could walk on dry land and used their long necks to browse on trees, just as giraffes do today.

Whatever the truth about their lifestyle, the sauropods included some of the most famous and most spectacular animals which have ever

lived. *Diplodocus* was a staggering 27 metres (87 feet) long. It lived in North America about 150 million years ago. Even larger was a dinosaur known as *Ultrasaurus*. Fossils of this creature were found in the United States in 1979. They proved that the animal was over 32 metres (100 feet) long and weighed more than 140 tons. *Ultrasaurus* was the largest animal ever to have lived.

The many and diverse species of dinosaur were the most successful animals on Earth for 150 million years. They evolved to huge sizes and many different shapes. Despite this success, they suddenly vanished from the earth as if they had never existed. Every single dinosaur became extinct some time around 65 million years ago.

Many people have tried to invent a theory to explain this dramatic event. It has been suggested that a virulent disease wiped out the dinosaurs, or that a change in climate created conditions deadly to them. However, scientists now realize that vast numbers of other animals died out at the same time as the dinosaurs. Flying reptiles, sea reptiles and many microscopic animals became extinct. Clearly whatever happened was both dramatic and catastrophic.

Perhaps the most popular theory to explain the mass extinctions is that they occurred when a gigantic meteor struck the Earth. If such a meteor, which would have been the size of a city, did collide with Earth it would have had far reaching effects. Vast amounts of steam and dust would have been thrown into the atmosphere. This would have cut off the light of the sun from the surface of the planet, killing plants and the animals which ate them. Smaller animals such as birds, mammals and lizards might have been able to find enough food and would have survived the catastrophe.

Although this theory explains much about the mass extinctions, it does not fit all the available evidence. Many scientists think that the extinctions were caused by less dramatic events and favour climatic change. Whatever caused the mass extinctions of 65 million years ago, we can be sure that the dinosaurs became extinct. Or can we?

For nearly a hundred years, reports from the Congo Basin in central Africa have seemed to indicate that a dinosaur might still exist. The earliest tales about the giant creature were told by the local people. The various tribes knew the monster by a number of different names, of which the most common was mokele mbembe. Most of the Europeans who travelled through the area in the last century heard stories about the monster, but refused to believe them.

However, one man, a German explorer

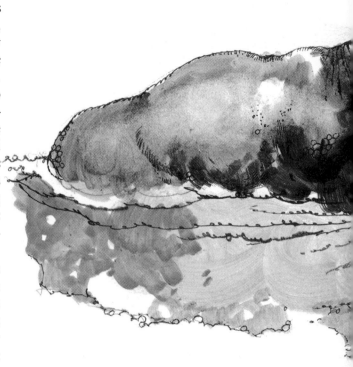

Only a very few outsiders have claimed to have seen the mokele mbembe, but many locals say that they have come across the huge and ferocious beast.

named Captain Freiherr von Stein zu Lausnitz, recorded many of the stories he heard about the mokele mbembe. In 1913, he summed up the tales when he wrote that "The animal is said to be of a brownish-gray color with a smooth skin, its size approximating that of an elephant . . . It is said to have a long and very flexible neck and only one tooth, but a very long one . . . A few spoke about a long muscular tail . . . It is said to climb the shore even at daytime in search of food; its diet is said to be entirely vegetable. The preferred plant was shown to me; it is a kind of liana with a milky sap and applelike fruits." Most reports stated that the monster was about 16 metres (50 feet) long. Von Stein was even shown the tracks of this animal, but he remained unconvinced of its existence.

The publicity surrounding these reports, and

ferocious mokele mbembe continued to trickle in. In 1920 a Frenchman named Lepage returned from an expedition into Africa. He said that the mokele mbembe had charged at him and that he had only just escaped with his life. Unfortunately, Monsieur Lepage disappeared after making his report and many people thought that the story was a fake.

In 1932 the highly-respected researcher Ivan T. Sanderson had a close encounter with an animal which may have been the mokele mbembe. While travelling in a canoe on an African river, Sanderson was shocked to hear a loud roar. Seconds later a monstrous animal rose out of the water. Sanderson guessed that the head was as large as a fully-grown hippopotamus. The scientist and his expedition left the area at high speed.

The most recent attempt to find the mokele mbembe was made by Dr Roy Mackal of Chicago University and James Powell. In 1981 they travelled to the Congo to investigate the reports. The two men were not convinced by tales of a living dinosaur. They only wanted to discover "whether reports of the mokele mbembe refer to a myth or real animals . . . and to obtain as much information as to their nature and habitat as possible".

The expedition spent many weeks in the Congo jungles and the two men returned convinced that the mokele mbembe was a real animal, though they had not seen one themselves. In 1987 Mackall announced his intention of returning to the Congo in search of this elusive monster.

similar tales, caused a sensation in Europe. The description of the mokele mbembe seemed to fit that of sauropod dinosaurs. Both the supposed African monster and the long-extinct giants had long necks and tails, ate only plants and lived in water.

The idea that a dinosaur might actually still be alive was dismissed by scientists, but not by those who knew central Africa. Unexplored regions covering many thousands of square miles exist in this area of Africa. Impenetrable swamps and thick jungle cover the region and have never been visited. There is plenty of room in Africa for large numbers of huge animals to live without ever being seen by man.

Reports of sightings of the massive and

The Komodo Dragons

In Indonesia, between Timor and Java, is a string of exotic islands known as the Sunda Archipelago. During the last century these islands were covered by dense jungle and ruled by the Sultan of Bima. They remained largely unknown to Europeans. Local farmers and fishermen who lived in the region stated that giant reptilian monsters lurked in the island jungles, but no scientists seriously believed them.

Everything changed in 1912 when an unlucky airman flew over the island of Komodo. Suddenly his aircraft broke down, and the pilot was forced to crashland on the island. Only slightly injured, the man managed to scramble from the cockpit. As he looked about him, he was startled to find himself confronted by a number of huge reptiles. The monsters circled the wreckage of the aircraft as the terrified man ran off.

This report of a real-life monster caused a local Dutch official to mount an expedition to the island. He came back with two dead giant reptiles and the existence of the "Komodo dragon", as it was known, was proved.

The monstrous reptile is a giant species of monitor. These lizards are common throughout Africa, Asia and Australia, but most species are less than two metres (six feet) long. The Komodo dragon measures up to four metres (13 feet) and is enormously powerful. Some locals report seeing monsters up to eight metres (26 feet) in length.

Even at a length of four metres (13 feet) the Komodo dragon is a fearsome beast. The monster has tremendously strong jaws and is very fierce. It will attack wild pigs, deer and horses voraciously. Only a few savage bites from the reptile are needed for its prey to fall dead. The dragon is then able to tear flesh from the carcass, reducing it to a skeleton in a matter of minutes.

When hungry, the Komodo dragon is not particular about what it eats. Many reports speak of these giant reptiles attacking each other and fighting to the death. The victor then eats the vanquished. The dragon has even been known to attack and eat people. Such attacks are rare because nobody lives on the island of

Above: a fine example of the Komodo dragon, the largest lizard on earth.

Right: the stranded pilot was horrified to see the monsters surrounding him.

Komodo, and only the few visitors to the island are threatened.

The Komodo dragons are known to flick their long tongues in and out of their mouths almost constantly. This enables them to "taste" the air in much the way that other animals smell. So sensitive is the tongue, that the Komodo dragon is able to find its prey from a considerable distance. When the dragon is grappling with a victim, the delicate tongue is protected within a special sheath of skin inside the mouth.

The Indonesian government has recently introduced strict protection for the Komodo dragon. Only specially licensed individuals are allowed to hunt the animal. In fact, the growing reputation of the animal for its ferocity has meant that tourism to the island has declined and the dragon is being left in peace once again.

The Komodo dragon is by no means the largest monitor lizard ever to have lived. Scientists have recently discovered the fossils of an even larger relative of the Komodo dragon which lived in Australia a few thousand years ago. This fearsome monster was seven metres (23 feet) in length and was an even more powerful hunter than the dragon is today.

Sucuriju

The longest snake recognized by science is the reticulated python which lives in Malaysia. The largest specimen ever recorded measured ten metres (32 feet 9 inches). However, there are stories of giant snakes many times larger than this. If the reports are true, these beasts would be monsters indeed.

The huge serpents are said to live in the dense rainforests of South America. The rainforest is incredibly rich in wildlife. There are probably more species of animals and plants here than anywhere else on Earth. Each year new species are being discovered. These forests cover thousands of square kilometres and vast areas have never been visited by explorers.

The possible existence of such a beast was first brought to the notice of the outside world before the First World War by Colonel Percy Fawcett, an experienced traveller who had mapped large areas of the rainforest for the Brazilian government. The explorer states that as he and his party travelled down the Rio Negro by canoe in 1907, they felt their craft strike an obstruction. Thinking he had hit a sandbank, Fawcett peered into the river. He was terrified to see the body of an immense snake gliding under the canoe.

The massive snake climbed on to the bank of the river and raised its fearsome head to gaze at Fawcett. Grabbing his rifle, Fawcett shot the snake, smashing its spine. He later measured the body as well as he could. It was a staggering 20 metres (65 feet) in length.

From talking to locals, Fawcett learned that an even larger snake had been killed some time earlier near the Rio Paraguay. He was also shown tracks in the forest indicating a snake at least twice the size of the one he had measured. The natives knew the monster by the name of sucuriju.

When he returned from his exploration, Fawcett eagerly reported his giant snake. Nobody believed him. Fawcett was ridiculed in the press and scientists accused him of fabricating the whole story. Fawcett was incensed. He was believed when he measured a river or mountain, but not when he measured a snake.

Fawcett returned to the jungles where, in 1925, he vanished without trace.

Though Fawcett had been disbelieved, other travellers in the rainforest continued to report the presence of a giant snake. In 1947 a government expedition pushed through the forest to make peace with the warlike Chavantes tribe. On their journey they found a sucuriju which measured 23 metres (75 feet). The members of the expedition noticed that local Indians did not think that such a huge size was at all unusual.

But the greatest snake ever reported was that stumbled upon by a Brazilian army patrol in 1954. Marching through the rainforest, the men were startled by the sudden appearance of a gigantic snake head rearing up out of the foliage. Thoroughly frightened, the men pumped machine gun bullets into it. Having killed the beast, they then measured it. The animal was 37 metres (120 feet) in length, four times the length of the largest snake recognized by science.

The truth of reports of the sucuriju has never been firmly established. The animal is rarely encountered, but is usually found in the depths of the tropical jungle many days journey from the nearest town. Under such conditions it is impossible for witnesses to carry the rotting carcass home for scientific examination. All they can do is measure it and take photographs. Invariably scientists refuse to believe such tales, even when they come from men as respected as Percy Fawcett.

The sudden appearance of the giant snake startled the soldiers. One of them opened fire, killing the snake.

WILD MEN

The Yeti

The people who lived in the Himalayas have no doubt that the mountains are the home of a hideous monster. Said to be half man and half beast, this creature strides across the snowfields and the valleys searching for food and threatening all who meet it. The monster is called the yeti.

Tales of this man-beast have been common in the mountains for centuries, but they did not come to the notice of the outside world until the

A Nepalese yakherd gives a description of the yeti to Charles Wylie, who has devoted much time to the study of the mysterious animal.

late 19th century. In 1889, Colonel W. Waddell found giant footprints in the snow. Each print was 47 centimetres (18 inches) long and they were regularly spaced. Waddell could not imagine what animal could have made these tracks, but locals told him they belonged to a yeti. In 1936 Frank Smythe found similar tracks. His local guides took one look at the footprints and refused to go any further.

However, such sightings of footprints caused little excitement among the general public. It was in 1951 that the yeti began to be taken seriously. On 8 November, a mountaineering party led by Eric Shipton was moving across the Menlung Glacier when they came across a line of strange footprints. About the same size as those seen by Waddell, the tracks ran for about a mile. Shipton followed the trail and carefully inspected the tracks. They were clearly man-like, but too large to have been made by a man. Choosing one of the clearest prints, Shipton took a photograph.

When the picture was printed in the newspapers, it caused a sensation. The yeti suddenly became news and everybody wanted to know more about the mystery monster. In 1954 the *Daily Mail* sent a special expedition to the Himalayas to hunt the yeti. But, apart from a few footprints, the expedition found nothing.

Despite such failures, interest in the yeti increased and occasional reports continued to come in. Older tales of the monster were re-examined and some remarkable incidents came to light. In 1921 Lt Colonel Howard-Bury had actually seen what he thought was a yeti. He said that the creature walked upright across the snow. Unfortunately he only saw the creature at a distance and could not make out any details.

Sightings of the yeti remained rare and inconclusive. Late one night in 1970 the climber Don Whillans saw a distant figure bounding along in the moonlight. He watched the creature for about 20 minutes while it pulled at some tree branches. Then the creature ran up a mountain slope and vanished among some rocks. Whillans thought that the creature looked like a large ape. The Sherpa guides with Whillans were unnerved by the encounter and seemed to be scared and on edge for several days.

In 1975, a Polish mountaineer named Janusz Tomaszczuk was walking through the Himalayas when he twisted his ankle. Hobbling down a hillside, he suddenly found himself face to face with a large ape several inches taller than himself and with arms reaching to its knees.

Screaming in fright, Tomaszczuk scared the creature away.

In 1953 and 1954 European explorers discovered that two mountain monasteries, Pangboche and Khumjang, had objects claimed to be yeti scalps in their possession. In 1960 the Khumjang Monastery allowed their scalp to be examined by scientists. Though appearing to be genuine at first sight, the scalp was later declared to be a clever fake made from wild goat skin. The potentially conclusive proof was discredited.

Though the continuing sightings and footprints seem to indicate the existence of a large two-legged creature in the Himalayas they do

Thyangboche, where John Hunt was told about the yeti.

not provide much detail about the yeti itself. Europeans travel through the mountains relatively infrequently so they are unlikely to sight a yeti. The local tribesmen, however, say that they frequently come across the creature. Their descriptions give a clear picture of the elusive creature.

The tales told by local Sherpas are a mixture of myth and fact. For instance some say that if a yeti runs downhill its long hair falls over its eyes and it becomes lost. Such a feature is unlikely to occur in a real animal. However, several researchers have spent some time talking to Sherpas and have tried to disentangle myth from reality.

Above: Eric Shipton returns to Britain after his 1951 expedition. He presented evidence to the Royal Geographical Society which seemed to show the yeti really existed. His most famous piece of evidence was the photograph of a footprint (below).

There appear to be two, or possibly three, types of yeti. The smallest of these has been identified as a species of gibbon by investigators. The only problem with this identification is that gibbons are not known to live in India. Perhaps this means that there is an unknown species in the area. Other researchers think that the small yetis may simply be young or female specimens of the larger types.

A second type is known as the dzu teh. This is the largest of the yetis and is said to be covered by shaggy hair. It has been known to attack large animals such as yaks and cattle. In 1975, such a creature attacked a young Sherpa girl called Lhakpa Sherpani. The girl managed to escape, but the creature then pounced on her yaks and killed one. Some scientists think that the dzu teh may be the extremely rare blue bear.

The classic descriptions of the yeti, however, seem to describe a third type of animal. It is said to be just over two metres (seven feet) tall when it stands on its hind legs. However, it is usually seen moving on all fours. The short legs, long arms and muscular body are covered with thick brown fur. The head of the animal has less fur and rises to a point on the top of the skull. When shown pictures of other animals, Sherpas usually indicate an orang-utan or gorilla as resembling a yeti. Some locals say that the animal is a man-eater, but other reports indicate that it feeds on plants. Most Sherpas think that this animal lives in the dense forests which cover the mountain valleys and that it only rarely visits the snowfields.

The fact that the creature lives in the forests may explain why it is not often seen. Most researchers look for it in the snow region and in the dense forest it would be difficult to find such an animal. A forest habitat would also solve the problem of what yetis eat. There is plenty of food in the forest to support a population of yeti, but not in the snowfields.

These descriptions indicate that the yeti is a large ape. Scientists have found fossils of apes in the Himalayas which date back only a few thousand years. In southern China the fossils of a truly enormous ape, named *Gigantopithecus*, have been found. This huge beast was far larger than a modern gorilla and is thought to have been able to reach a height of nearly four metres (12 feet) if it stood on its hind feet. Perhaps the yeti is the descendant of these creatures.

The mountaineers led by Hillary (seated right) and Shipton (far left).

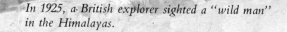

In 1925, a British explorer sighted a "wild man" in the Himalayas.

Early men confront ape men in a scene from the film Quest for Fire.

Paul Freeman with a cast from the footprint of a sasquatch he sighted in Washington State, USA.

The Sasquatch

In the western mountains of North America is said to live a most remarkable animal. It is described as being a giant human covered with hair. The beast has been seen by a large number of people and one man has even claimed to have taken a film of the creature. However, no firm evidence of the creature's existence has ever been produced. No scientist is certain that the creature is real. The wildman is known by its Indian name of sasquatch, or by its modern nickname of bigfoot.

During the 19th century, early explorers and travellers were told stories of the sasquatch by local Indians. Over the following years several white people saw the creature and reported the sightings to local newspapers. At the time, people thought the sasquatch was a normal man who had taken to a life in the woods and grown a hairy coat. It was not realized that the sasquatch might be a new species of man.

The stories of the sasquatch first became famous in the 1920s when two dramatic sightings were reported. The first occurred in the summer of 1922 when Fred Beck and some friends were prospecting near Mount St Helens, Washington State. According to his story, Beck came across a sasquatch one afternoon and shot it. Immediately several other sasquatches appeared and chased after Beck.

The frightened hunter ran back to his log cabin and told his friends what had happened. They locked themselves in. Minutes later the enraged sasquatches arrived. They tried to batter their way into the cabin using branches and large rocks. After several hours the creatures left. Beck and his companions fled the area and never returned.

Two years later, a lumberjack named Albert Ostman returned from the woods of British Columbia with an even stranger tale. He said that he had woken up one night to find himself being carried by a large sasquatch. The creature carried Ostman for several miles until they reached the sasquatch's family. The group was made up of an adult male, adult female and two young. Ostman was kept captive for several days, but he eventually escaped.

Once these spectacular reports had made the sasquatch famous, many other people began to report encounters with the monster. The many sightings reveal a consistent pattern both to the appearance and behaviour of the creature.

A typical report was that made in 1955 by William Roe who was out hunting in British Columbia. He was hiding in a bush when a female sasquatch approached. Roe reported that the beast was about two metres (six feet) tall and covered with hair. As he watched, the creature squatted down and started nibbling at a bush. Suddenly the sasquatch spotted Roe. She stood up and slowly walked away.

In most reports, the sasquatch is described as being up to three metres (ten feet) tall. It is said to be massively built with strong muscular arms. The creatures seem to be timid and usually retreat whenever they meet a human.

By the mid-1960s the evidence for the sasquatch was plentiful and interesting. It consisted of many eyewitness encounters and the finding of hundreds of tracks in the forests. But in 1967 a man named Roger Patterson produced a film which he claimed showed a sasquatch he had come across in California. When the film was viewed by scientists it clearly showed a hairy upright figure walking slowly across a clearing and into some trees.

The film was hailed as evidence that the sasquatch existed, and specialists began to study the film for evidence of a fraud. It soon became clear that the film had not been tampered with, but suspicions grew that the sasquatch was really a man in a fur suit.

The film was subjected to complicated scientific analysis. Some scientists felt that the creature in the film was not moving as such a beast should. Its stride was the wrong length and its bodily proportions did not fit together properly. Other specialists discounted these objections and pointed instead to the way the muscles clearly moved under the skin and the realistic gait, both of which would be very difficult to fake. Scientific opinion was divided. The situation is best summed up by Don Abbot who stated "It is about as hard to believe the film is faked as it is to admit that such a creature really lives."

The man–beasts of Asia and America appear to be different creatures. Above left: these yeti tracks photographed in the Himalayas are quite unlike the sasquatch print (bottom left) from America and the cast of a mysterius footprint (below right) found in Russia. The wealth of evidence for the sasquatch has enabled a local artist to create a statue of the elusive creature (above right).

No sooner had the sensation caused by the Patterson film died down than an even more sensational announcement was made. In 1969 Frank Hansen announced that he owned a frozen corpse of the hairy apeman. He later claimed that he had shot the creature in the Minnesota woods. Hansen kept the body in a block of ice in a deep freeze and travelled to various fairs charging an admission fee to those who wished to see it.

Two scientists, Ivan Sanderson and Bernard Huevelmans, inspected the corpse. They photographed, sketched and measured it, though Hansen refused to melt the block of ice encasing the corpse. The two men published a report claiming the discovery of a new species of man. Other scientists remained sceptical, especially when Hansen refused to hand the corpse over for inspection.

Suspicion grew that the corpse was little more than a rubber model. Controversy raged in the press and in scientific circles, but without being able to inspect the corpse neither side could prove its case. To this day nobody is sure whether the ''iceman'', as it has become known, is a genuine creature or a fake.

Much the same could be said for the sasquatch itself. Hundreds of people claim to have seen the beast. The evidence of the eye-witnesses and of tracks is impressive. However, without an actual specimen to examine, scientists will not accept that the sasquatch exists.

Frank Hansen said he shot a man-beast in Minnesota, though he later denied the story.

A still from the controversial film shot by Roger Patterson in 1967. Patterson claims that this shows a real sasquatch. Others are not too sure.
(Photo Patterson/Gimlin, © 1968 Dahinden Fortean Picture Library).

A photograph of the "Minnesota Ice Man".

The Almas

Fifty thousand years ago, Europe was in the grip of the ice age. Sheets of ice thousands of feet thick covered the landscape. The northern regions shivered in perpetual winter and bleak, treeless tundra dominated the landscape. Beyond this region lay vast forests of pines and firs. In these forests lurked two remarkable animals which are now usually considered to be long extinct. Recent evidence suggests they may still be alive in the forests of Siberia.

The creatures in question are the woolly mammoth and Neanderthal man, a close relative of modern man. The two creatures lived side by side and had a profound effect upon each other.

The woolly mammoth, known to science as *Mammuthus primigenius*, stood some 3.5 metres (11 feet) tall and was covered in long, red hair. The mammoth roamed through the forests eating twigs and pine needles. Superbly adapted to the cold climate, the mammoth survived for more than 300,000 years. During the periods of warm weather between each ice age the mammoths moved to bleak northern forests where they survived in small numbers until the cold weather returned.

Neanderthal man, and more especially his successor Cromagnon man, hunted the mammoth ruthlessly. A mammoth kill would provide the humans with a wide variety of material. The meat of the mammoth was eaten while the hairy skin could be cut up to provide several warm cloaks to keep the winter chill at bay. Even the bones and ivory of the mammoth could be used to make tools and weapons.

When the final ice age ended about 15,000 years ago the mammoth is presumed to have become extinct. However, there is no real reason to believe that the mammoth did not retreat to the cold forests where it had spent previous warm spells. Earlier this century evidence emerged which suggests that this might have happened. The mighty mammoth could still survive today.

The vast Siberian forest covers about 7,300,000 square kilometres (3,000,000 square miles). Very few people live in the largely

Neanderthal men hunting mammoths in Europe about 100,000 years ago. Do such scenes still occur in Siberia?

unexplored wilderness. A few mining camps have been established near mineral deposits, and some native hunters make a living in the forests, but otherwise the region is uninhabited. It would not be difficult for a creature even as large as a mammoth to remain hidden in such an area.

Several local tales speak of a large animal living in the forests, but more specific was the account of a grizzled old Russian trapper who told his tale to a Frenchman visiting Russia in 1920. According to the Russian he was in a remote region of the forests when he came across huge tracks belonging to a four-legged animal. Each footprint was 60 centimetres (two feet) across. Intrigued, the man decided to follow the trail.

After pushing through the forest for several days, the man suddenly came across his quarry. He thought he recognized it from pictures he had seen. "It was a huge elephant with big white tusks, very curved. It had fairly long hair." The hunter could not imagine what an elephant was doing in Siberia, as far as he knew elephants were only found in tropical regions. He knew nothing about prehistoric mammoths.

One point which seems to indicate that the man may have been telling the truth stands out. He claims to have met the mammoth in the forest. At the time of the encounter scientists thought that mammoths lived on open plains. It is only recently that their true lifestyle has been discovered.

Other strange reports from people living in Asia refer to a creature known as the alma. The stories of almas come most frequently from mountainous regions, such as the Pamirs. They speak of a man-like creature which seems very similar to Neanderthal man. In January 1988 the Russian government announced that it was

sending a special expedition into Siberia to investigate these reports.

The locals who regularly encounter almas have no doubt that the creatures exist. The almas are considered to be inferior humans, rather than animals, and some locals even claim to have married almas.

Though descriptions vary slightly, the typical alma bears a close resemblance to Neanderthal man. The alma is said to be about the same size and shape; the face, however, is very different. A prominent ridge of bone runs above the eyes and the nose is wide and flat. The alma is said to be able to use stones and branches as tools and seems to understand fire.

If Neanderthal man does still exist in the form of the alma, it would completely change the picture scientists have built up of the evolution of man and his near relatives.

THE FIENDS

Demons and Devils

Many religions understand the concepts of good and evil. The material world is often seen as a battleground between these ultimate forces of the Universe. According to the Christian Bible, the spirit of evil is a rebel angel known as Satan, Lucifer or the Devil.

The Bible states that, after God had created the Universe and His angels, Satan became consumed with pride. He was the brightest and best angel in heaven, and felt that he was as strong and powerful as God. Sometimes he even put God to the test. Finally, the growing pride of Satan became too great; the Bible tells us there was war in heaven between the angels. God threw the Devil down to hell, into the chains of darkness (*2 Peter Chapter 2*).

Having rebelled against God, Satan could no longer live in heaven. But as Satan himself declares in the Book of Job, he could go to and fro in the Earth and walk up and down in it. Here he was free to tempt humans to join him in evil. Playing upon such motives as envy, greed and pride, Satan is believed by Christians to work constantly upon individuals in the hope of dragging them down to hell.

When he left heaven, the Devil was thought to have taken a number of lesser evil angels with him. The lesser beings believed to be serving Satan are known as demons. They are said to roam continuously around the world causing misery and evil. Some mediaeval scholars estimated that there were more than 133 million demons in the world, though it is not clear how the figure was arrived at. The names of the chief demons were said to be Beelzebub, Asmodeus and Baliar. Though these demons could change their shape, they often had animal features, such as horns or cloven hooves, so humans might recognize them when they came to Earth.

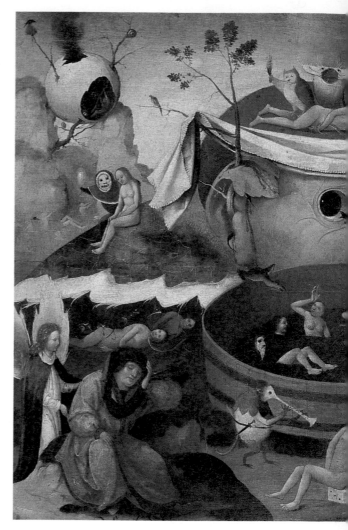

This belief in the Devil has had a profound effect on Christian thought and beliefs. During the Middle Ages, theologians and monks spent long hours discussing the nature of Satan and his powers. It was hoped that by knowing the Devil, humans could resist his temptations and defeat evil. In some instances this led to a belief that holy men and women should retreat from the world to avoid the taint of evil: some became hermits, others joined monasteries.

The most extreme form of this movement away from the world came in the 6th century in the Middle East. A group of monks, determined to escape the evil of the world, climbed to the top of pillars and stayed there. Their only contacts with the world were the food supplies regularly hoisted to the holy men. St Simeon the Younger stayed on the top of his pillar for 45 years until he died.

established in popular belief. He was considered to have power over all earthly matters, but could only claim souls if they were willingly surrendered to him. It was, therefore, believed that individuals could strike pacts with the Devil in which souls were exchanged for worldly goods. At Bungay in Suffolk, a huge, prehistoric stone stands in the churchyard. Locals believe that if a person dances around the stone 12 times, Satan himself will appear. Having summoned the Devil, many people are believed to have arranged deals with the fiend. Seven hundred years ago, near Aberystwyth in Wales, a woman needed to cross a rushing stream. The Devil agreed to build a bridge, if he could have

Above: this macabre scene shows the traditional view of hell as depicted by a 16th-century Dutch painter.

Right: an engraving showing the Devil being cast out of heaven.

The majority of Christians, however, had to earn their living as farmers, craftsmen or soldiers. They believed that they remained in peril from the temptations of the Devil. In 1638, for instance, a stranger strode into the village of Widecombe-in-the-Moor, Devon. The well-dressed man went to the church to attend Sunday service. One of the villagers said that he glanced at the man and was horrified to see that he had cloven hooves. Seconds later a devastating bolt of fire slammed into the church causing immense damage.

Beliefs concerning the Devil became increasingly complex. The character of Satan became

Satan and the Saint

At Mayfield in Sussex, locals tell a story of an encounter between Satan and Saint Dunstan, Archbishop of Canterbury between 961 and 979. According to the tale Dunstan practised metal work as a hobby. While he was working at his forge one day a beautiful young woman came to see him. Dunstan, however, recognized the girl as the Devil. He spun round and gripped the girl's nose in his red hot tongs. The girl screamed in pain and changed shape to that of the Devil. Dunstan and Satan wrestled for some time, but the Devil finally escaped and fled the district.

A scene from the Swedish film Witches, *made in the 1920s, shows a nun at prayer while a demon looks on, waiting his chance.*

the soul of the first to cross it. The woman agreed and a bridge appeared. She then sent her dog running across the bridge to cheat the Devil of a human soul.

According to the old tales, offering a bargain with the Devil was a risky business. All too often Satan would appear and claim his prize, whisking an unfortunate soul off to hell. A few wily individuals, however, were able to escape such dangerous pacts. A tailor in Clitheroe, Lancashire, exchanged his soul for four wishes. When Satan arrived to claim the tailor's soul, the man had one wish left. He wished that "that dun horse carried you off to hell where you could trouble me no more". With a terrible shriek of rage, the Devil leapt on the horse and galloped off. The village inn was promptly renamed "The Devil upon Dun".

Trouble with the Devil did not always follow

Women accused of witchcraft could be tried by "swimming". If, when thrown into water with hands and feet tied, the woman sank she was innocent.

from voluntary arrangements. In the 11th century, Piers Shonks is said to have killed a dragon in Hertfordshire. The Devil then appeared and swore to take Shonks' soul whether he was buried inside or outside a church. When Shonks died, he outwitted Satan by having his body bricked up in the church wall.

In these traditional stories, the Devil appears as the enemy of God and everything that is good. He is, however, not all-powerful and can be outsmarted on occasion. The views of the Church were quite different. The clergy thought that any agreement with the Devil was an entirely evil act which should be punished in the most frightful way possible.

Church authorities considered that witchcraft was the most awful form of agreement with the Devil. Many clergymen in the period 1400–1700 believed that witchcraft was a real evil within society. Thousands of people were thought to participate in the wicked activities. Whenever a witch was caught she, or he, could expect little mercy and would be executed.

Witchcraft was equated with devil-worship and the clergymen extracted confessions which seemed to support the idea. Witches declared that during their ceremonies they parodied Christian worship. The cross was trodden into the dust and new converts were "baptised" with a foul, stinking liquid. However, such declarations were often made under torture and are unreliable. Exactly how widespread witchcraft was in these years is unknown, but it seems certain that most of the thousands of people executed as witches were innocent.

Another form of supposed satanic activity is possession. This occurs when Satan, or one of his demons, is believed to take control of a human. The person's body is then ruled by the demon. At times, the demon may cause the person to behave normally, but it can also force the human body to commit evil acts or to fall into convulsions and trances. On such occasions the face of the possessed is said to be twisted into an expression of rage and pain.

In the 1880s at Ars, France, a man strode into the church with his wife. She was raging and shouting in an unknown language. The man told the priest that his wife often suffered in this way. The priest suspected the woman was possessed and recommended the man to take his wife to see the bishop. Suddenly a coarse voice rang out "if I only had the power of Christ, I would drag you to hell".

"So you know Christ" declared the priest and dragged the protesting woman to the altar. There he placed a holy reliquary on the woman's head. She promptly collapsed. When the woman regained consciousness she was quite normal and never suffered such fits again.

On 23 June 1920, Father Pier Paolo conducted an exorcism on a woman in Italy. She had been ill for several years, falling into fits and raving incoherently. At the height of the exorcism, a strange voice was heard to mutter "I am going." The woman was cured.

It is the more horrific aspects of demons which have become the centre of attention in recent years. Though many of the symptoms of possession can now be explained as mental illness of various types, many people cling to the older explanation. Clergymen are being called upon by members of the public to perform exorcisms with increasing frequency.

The interest in the Devil and his demons has been reflected in, and perhaps encouraged by, numerous films dealing with demonic possession and devil-worship. Perhaps the best-known of these films was *The Exorcist*, released in 1973. The film centred on the struggle between an exorcist

A vision of Lucifer, the prince of hell, with lesser demons, based upon descriptions contained in the Bible.

and a demon for the possession of a 12-year-old girl. The storyline drew upon traditional beliefs as well as the imagination of the writer.

Interest in Satan, if not actual belief, continues to the present day. But most people believe it is a dangerous practice which should be left alone.

Left: this painting, The Bewitched, *by the Spanish artist Goya, clearly depicts the horror suffered by the bewitched or the possessed.*

The Bells

It has long been believed that Satan and his demons are afraid of the sound of bells. It was for this reason that church bells were tolled at a funeral. It was hoped that if the demons were frightened away the soul of the dead stood a better chance of getting to heaven.

Goblins and Gremlins

In many areas of Western Europe, countryfolk once believed that lurking in quiet places were fiendish little creatures known as goblins. Though goblins might be helpful on occasion, they could also cause great misery to anyone unfortunate enough to encounter them. It was usually thought best to avoid them.

Goblins, according to the few people who claim to have seen them, are hideous little beings. They appear as little men, rarely more than knee-high to an adult human, with ugly faces and straggly hair. They are said to be dressed in scruffy clothes, which are often green or brown in colour.

The traditional homes of goblins were to be found deep in forests. Usually goblins preferred to live in caves, hills or simply in underground homes. In Derbyshire, for instance, a large prehistoric burial mound was said to be the home of a goblin named Hob Hurst.

This particular goblin enjoyed making shoes, but had a curious habit of then throwing the shoes out of windows. Apparently a cobbler in Dore, in Yorkshire, had an encounter with Hob Hurst in the last century. If the man left good shoe leather in his workroom at night, he would find it made into fine shoes the following morning. Hoping to take advantage of Hob Hurst, the man left a huge amount of leather in his workroom. Next morning a massive pile of shoes lay outside his window and Hob Hurst never returned. Though useful, such goblins were also mischievous, delighting in making workrooms untidy and hiding tools.

More obviously wicked were the goblins which lived near Lanercost in Cumbria. One night, late last century, a man was riding home from the local inn. Suddenly a group of goblins rushed out from the woods and leapt at him. The little men dragged the man from his horse and beat him. Then the ugly figures began to drag the man back to their underground home. As the man struggled against his loathsome attackers, his Bible fell from his pocket. The goblins took one look at the holy book and fled.

In nearby Bassenthwaite, it seems that two boys stumbled upon the home of some goblins.

The youngsters were digging into a small hill, when they found what appeared to be the roof of a little house. Excavating further, the boys found slate tiles and a gutter. At this point, their mother called the boys in for dinner. When the lads returned to their work, they could find neither the hole, nor the little house. Only their spades lay on the side of the hill.

A short time later the boys' father saw two goblins emerging from the little hill where the boys had been digging. They were dressed in green and had the traditional pointed ears and long hair. The farmer was accompanied by his ferocious guard dog and he sent the hound bounding forwards to attack the goblins. One of the little beings turned and spoke some strange words to the advancing dog. Immediately the dog turned and ran whimpering back to its master. After this, the farmer left the goblins alone.

Sightings of goblins have been reported only rarely this century. The reasons for this are not known, but it may be that fewer people are working as farmers and shepherds. If fewer people are in the countryside, there is, of course, less chance of anyone saying they have seen or met goblins.

However, the modern technological age seems to have given the mischievous goblins new opportunities to cause trouble. One particular type of goblin has achieved great fame as a result of its activities.

During the Second World War, the men of the Royal Air Force said that they were suffering from the attentions of strange little men. Dressed in red jackets and tight breeches, the strange creatures were soon named gremlins. The gremlins were thought to live in burrows dug into the grass surrounding wartime air bases.

The pilots soon joked about gremlins loving to fly, and taking any opportunity to sneak aboard an aircraft. Unfortunately, it seemed that the gremlins could not control their love of trouble. They would often cause instruments or engines to go wrong when they were in perfect working order.

During the summer of 1940 mass formations of German aircraft thundered over the English

A charming illustration of a cobbler and his wife watching the goblins which have been helping the cobbler with his work.

coast to rain bombs down upon cities and military bases. Squadrons of young British pilots flew their fighter planes up to meet the enemy aircraft and try to shoot them down. As the Spitfires and Hurricanes climbed into the air, the gremlins might make themselves known. An engine would fail, or a control suddenly jam. The pilot would be forced to return to base, saying resignedly that he had a gremlin on board.

As time passed, it was said that gremlins were tinkering with land-based equipment. Tele-phones, radars, radios and even cooking stoves began, apparently, to suffer from their activities. Soon any failure of RAF equipment was blamed in a semi-serious way upon the gremlins. This superstition has spread rapidly with gremlins being blamed for any mechanical failure wher-ever it occurred.

The Worshippers of Kali

Of all the religious cults and sects that have existed on Earth, few can have been as deadly or terrible as the Thugs, a small sect of the worshippers of Kali. This murderous religion was active for centuries in India, being most popular in the northern areas.

Thuggee, as the religion was called, was an hereditary sect with complicated and precise rituals. The goddess of the Thugs was Kali, a goddess of Hindu mythology. Kali is depicted with four arms. In one she holds a sword and in another a severed head. She wears earrings made of corpses and a necklace of skulls. This horrific deity is the Hindu goddess of death and destruction.

The Thugs believed that the greatest act of devotion they could offer to Kali was murder. They formed themselves into bands under recognized leaders and killed wholesale. In the course of a lifetime's career, a Thug might commit more than a thousand murders. Each murder was carried out to a precise plan.

The Thugs would wander the highways of India in groups. When they came across another group of travellers journeying in the same direction, the Thugs would suggest that the two groups joined together in case of attacks by bandits, which were not uncommon. As soon as this offer was accepted a group of Thugs would be sent ahead to dig the graves.

When the main group arrived at the killing ground each Thug would try to position himself behind a member of the other party. At a signal from the Thug leader the killing would begin. Each Thug carried a long handkerchief weighted with a coin. He deftly flicked this around his

The dreaded Thugs murdered thousands of victims by strangulation.

victim's neck and pulled it tight. With a flick of his wrist, an experienced Thug could kill a man in seconds.

As soon as the victims were dead, their bodies were stripped and their belongings rifled. Anything of value was taken. The bodies were at once buried in a well hidden grave. The Thugs then bought a small quantity of sugar and ate it as part of a religious service dedicated to Kali. The ceremony over, the Thugs moved on to look for fresh victims.

During the 1820s Colonel Sleeman, an officer of the East India Company, began to suspect the existence of this secret religion. He investigated reports of disappearing travellers and slowly uncovered the true horror of Thuggee. Sleeman estimated that about 10,000 people were murdered by Thugs every year. His investigations

led to a campaign by the British to destroy Thuggee.

A few Thugs were caught and, under threat of death, revealed the identities of other Thugs. One British official was staggered to discover that one killing ground lay just 200 metres (220 yards) from his office. Hundreds of people had been murdered and buried at the site without any suspicion being aroused. By 1848 the religion had been destroyed as an organized cult.

The Thug

The revelations of the true extent of the Thuggee cult caused a sensation both in India and Britain, where their activities were not even suspected. So great was the fame of the Thugs that people in Britain began to call any violent person a thug. Today, the word could be defined as a "brutal lout", a far cry from the religious murderers of India.

The Bogeymen

"Be quiet, or the bogeyman will get you." Thousands of parents have spoken these words to noisy children in the hope of frightening them into silence. The bogeyman with which the child is threatened is a hideous, evil creature which likes nothing better than to carry off young children so that they are never seen again. However, the bogeyman does not really exist. He is simply an invented monster which allows parents to threaten their children.

Many countries have their own particular type of bogeyman, a monster invented to frighten naughty children. In Scotland there was said to be a race of tiny, wizened old men. Known as bodachs, these creatures were particularly skilful at climbing down chimneys. In the days when every room had a fireplace, this gift would be extremely useful. The bodachs were able to creep down a chimney to a child's bedroom and kidnap the sleeping youngster.

The children who grow up in the Himalayan Mountains of Nepal and Tibet are threatened with a creature which many adults believe actually does exist. This is the yeti, which is discussed on page 36 of this book. The monster which is described to the children is more frightening than the real yeti. It is said to break into houses and carry off children for its supper.

Russian children were once particularly frightened by a creature known as Baba Yaga. This twisted, ugly old woman was said to live in a forest clearing near Moscow with her three daughters. Baba Yaga was able to sneak into houses at night and make off with any child who was not quietly tucked up in bed. She would then take them home and cook them for supper. In one story, a girl manages to escape from Baba Yaga by giving presents to the monstrous woman's pets. Baba Yaga never gave her pets anything, so the animals were very grateful and helped the girl to escape. Most children were not so lucky.

One of the most fantastic bogeymen was the Mantichora of India. This powerful and aggressive creature was said to have the body of a lion and the tail of a scorpion, complete with deadly sting. The head of the Mantichora was like that of a man, armed with rows of ferocious teeth. The monster would pounce on children and gobble them up.

Black Annis served a particular purpose for the parents of Scottish children. This ugly woman was said to live in a cave from which she kept a constant watch on the surrounding countryside. As soon as Black Annis saw a young child on its own and far from home, she would leap from her cave and grab the child. By frightening children with Black Annis, parents could ensure that the youngsters never strayed far from home.

Perhaps the most difficult of all "bogeymen" to recognize were the Dogai. These supernatural women were able to change their shape so that they resembled any natural object, such as a tree or stone. The Dogai lived on several islands in the Pacific. They were thought to enjoy luring children away from their homes. Once out of the earshot of parents, the child would be killed and eaten. Like Black Annis, the Dogai were probably invented to frighten children into staying at home.

In Japan, tales of a particularly savage water monster were used to stop young children swimming in dangerous rivers. The kappa was said to look like a large turtle with frog's legs and a monkey's head. Lurking beneath the waters, the kappa would grab hold of a swimmer's legs and drag them down to drown. Unlike most bogeymen, the kappa had a curious weakness. It loved to eat cucumbers. To ensure safety while swimming it was only necessary to throw a cucumber into the river first.

Parents in many other countries have invented monsters to frighten their children. Sometimes, the monsters were as vague as the bogeyman, who would attack children who were simply naughty. Others, such as Black Annis, were said to lurk in particular places. Usually these were locations which parents would rather children did not visit, such as dark forests or fast-flowing rivers. These bogeymen were deliberately invented monsters which humans used for their own purposes.

An imaginary bogeyman lurks ready to pounce on unwary children.

Trolls

Before the coming of Christianity to the wild northern forests of Scandinavia, the forests were the home of fearsome trolls. These frightening monsters were enormously powerful and extremely ugly. They took the form of men, but were some six metres (20 feet) tall and terribly misshapen. Some were described as having talons on their hands and long tails. Most trolls, however, were simply ugly and dirty. So dirty were they, that plants could grow in the mud stuck in their hair.

Trolls feature in many of the old stories of the northern lands. They are sometimes merely mischievous, delighting in causing mayhem by making horses stampede or blocking roads with trees. Some trolls, however, are clearly murderous. They would break into feasting halls late at night to kill men and steal their bodies for food.

The trolls were, however, restricted to the hours of darkness. If they did not return to their underground forest homes before dawn, they would turn into huge masses of stone. One hero managed to destroy a troll which was killing his friends by fighting it for several hours until sunlight struck the troll and killed it.

In most stories, trolls are said to be male, but in Iceland there seem to have been particularly violent female trolls. These fearsome creatures liked nothing better than to eat men. In one tale, a hero named Thorstein Oxleg kills a troll and is then attacked by the beast's mother. The strength of the female troll is stupendous and Thorstein realizes that he is losing the battle. In desperation, the hero promises to become a Christian if he wins the battle. At once, the troll becomes weak and Thorstein kills her with ease.

In some ways the tale of Thorstein Oxleg announces the end of the trolls. Once the Scandinavians became Christians, the trolls ceased to be such frightening creatures. They stopped threatening men and became little more than forest spirits.

A Scandinavian hero battles with a hideous and powerful troll; a monster said to lurk in the dark northern forests.

MONSTERS OF MYTH

Classical Monsters

The monsters of the ancient world were strange and fantastic creatures. Some were entirely fictitious animals of tremendous power. Others were at least half human and possessed frightening strength. A few monsters were probably simply misinterpretations of real creatures.

Whatever the monster, the fertile imagination of the ancient people gave them fantastic characteristics and set them in exciting tales. Most of these stories were concerned with violent emotions and towering passions.

The tale of the origin of the monster Scylla is typical of the passionate tales of ancient Greece. Scylla was a beautiful young maiden who came to the notice of Glaucus, a minor sea god. Glaucus visited the girl and fell in love with her. This aroused the jealousy of the enchantress Circe who was herself in love with Glaucus. Scylla, however, disliked Glaucus and would have nothing to do with him.

Glaucus became extremely angry and swore to take a terrible revenge upon the beautiful Scylla. Turning to Circe, who was only too happy to help, Glaucus asked for magical aid. Circe scattered special herbs into a pool where Scylla bathed each day. When the lovely maiden entered the pool, six necks erupted from her shoulders. Each neck carried a ferocious head which roared with savagery.

The hideously deformed Scylla fled from her home and dived into the waters between Sicily and Italy. Here she found a home in a large cave from which her heads projected. The ancient Greeks believed that Scylla still lurked in her underwater lair. Whenever dolphins or fish passed within reach, one of Scylla's monstrous heads would reach out and snap them up.

If a ship sailed too close to the cave, Scylla would spring forward and devour a sailor with each of her heads. The passage through the straits was made even more dangerous by Charybdis. This beast lay beneath the waves opposite the lair of Scylla. Three times each day Charybdis opened her mouth and swallowed the surrounding waters. Any ship hoping to pass between Sicily and Italy needed to steer a careful course to pass between these two frightful monsters.

Odysseus, one of the greatest Greek heroes, sailed through the straits, and lost several of his crew to the terrible jaws of Scylla. Odysseus also had an encounter with Circe, who had caused Scylla to become a monster. Circe changed Odysseus' crew into pigs, but the Greek hero outwitted her and persuaded her to restore his men. Another of the monsters of ancient Greece whom Odysseus met was a savage giant named Polyphemus, King of the Cyclops.

This monster was a huge man, possessed of tremendous strength, but he only had one eye. Polyphemus lived with the other cyclops on a remote island in the Mediterranean. During his long voyages, Odysseus and his crew arrived on this island and entered the cave where Polyphemus lived, but found themselves trapped. Polyphemus rolled a massive stone across the

The Greek monster Scylla had been a beautiful woman before she was cursed with six vicious heads.

An ancient bronze sculpture of Scylla, the sea monster of Greek mythology.

cave mouth whenever he entered or left, stopping them from escaping. When Polyphemus found two of Odysseus' men, he killed and ate them.

Realizing that he could only defeat the cyclops by cunning, Odysseus devised a plan. He offered Polyphemus a large cup of wine, and began to flatter the cyclops by praising his strength and ferocity. Odysseus then told the cyclops that his name was "Nobody". Polyphemus, lulled by wine and soft words, eventually fell asleep. Odysseus and his men then grabbed a huge spike which they had made from an olive tree left in the cave and plunged it into Polyphemus' eye.

The hideous monster leapt to his feet and started yelling in pain and rage. The other cyclops gathered outside the cave. But when they heard Polyphemus shouting "Nobody is attacking me," they left, thinking nothing was wrong.

Now utterly blind, Polyphemus could not find Odysseus and his men, but the Greeks were left with the problem of how to escape from the cave. Luckily Odysseus had another plan. He knew that Polyphemus opened the cave door each day to send his flock of sheep out to graze. Odysseus considered sneaking out at the same time as the sheep, but Polyphemus ran his hand over each sheep as it left to make sure it was not a man.

Odysseus, therefore, ordered his men to tie themselves to the underside of each sheep. When morning came, the cyclops opened the door. As each sheep passed he ran his hand over it, but failed to find the man hiding beneath. In this way, Odysseus and his men managed to escape and return to their ship.

The great hero Perseus was responsible for the death of perhaps the most dangerous of the Greek monsters, Medusa. Like Scylla, Medusa was originally a lovely woman. However, she offended the goddess Athena who became so enraged that she turned Medusa's hair to snakes and made her a monster with glaring eyes, whose gaze would turn anyone who saw her to stone. Medusa and her sisters retreated to a cave

which quickly became surrounded by statue-like figures: the petrified bodies of humans who had glimpsed Medusa.

Some years later Perseus grew up in Seriphos as a highly skilled, but very poor, young warrior. When King Polydectes announced his wedding plans, Perseus could not afford to buy a suitable present so he offered the king his services – he promised to do anything the king asked. So the king, wanting to be rid of him, asked for the head of Medusa. Fortunately Perseus was helped by the goddess Athena, who gave him a magic sword and a shiny shield.

After many adventures, Perseus arrived at the cave inhabited by Medusa. Walking backwards, he used his shield as a mirror so that he could attack Medusa without actually looking at her. With a single stroke he cut off her head and placed it in his bag. Perseus then returned to Seriphos, only to find King Polydectes persecuting his mother; the king had thought that Perseus would never return. Horrified at the king's action, Perseus pulled Medusa's head

The Giant Boar

One of the greatest legends of ancient Greece is the hunting of the Calydonian boar. A giant boar was sent by the angry goddess Artemis to ravage Calydon. King Oeneus gathered together all the great heroes of ancient Greece to help him hunt the boar.

A very similar story was told by the Celtic peoples of Britain some two thousand years later. In this version it is King Arthur who gathers together a host of heroes to hunt a giant boar named Twrch Trwyth. In this instance, the boar must be caught because of a silver comb which the boar has between its ears.

Odysseus flattered Polyphemus and gave him wine to drink until the giant became drunk and fell asleep. Odysseus then ordered his men to blind the monster.

One of Odysseus' crew escaping from the cave of the cyclops.

from his bag and turned the entire royal court to stone. Athena then claimed Medusa's head which she placed on her shield.

A monster of the Greeks which was part human and part animal was the terrible minotaur which lived on the island of Crete. This fearsome beast ate only fresh human flesh. King Minos of Crete kept this hideous monster in a maze, or labyrinth, which was so complicated that neither the minotaur nor anyone else could find their way out. In order to keep the minotaur fed, King Minos took youths from his subject cities and threw them into the labyrinth.

When Theseus, a young Athenian prince, heard of the next sacrifice he asked to be chosen for the minotaur. He was determined to kill the

monster and stop the bloodshed. When he arrived in Crete, Theseus met Ariadne, daughter of King Minos, who fell in love with him. She slipped a sword to Theseus before he was thrown into the labyrinth and told him to unwind a ball of string behind himself so that he could find his way out again.

Theseus followed the instructions of Ariadne. In the depths of the labyrinth, he met the terrible minotaur. At once the monster attacked Theseus, but the young man fought back with his sword. After a long and bloody battle, Theseus managed to kill the monster. He then turned around and followed his string out of the labyrinth. Theseus later married Ariadne and became King of Athens.

On the southern shores of the Mediterranean a civilization far older than that of Greece flourished. This was Egypt, which had frightening monsters of its own. Many of their temples and tombs were decorated with sculptures or paintings of a creature called the sphinx. A massive statue of a sphinx stands at Giza, beside the Great Pyramid. It is about 5,000 years old and is 58 metres (187 feet) long.

There is a story that the original sphinx used to wait beside a main highway and ask passers-by a riddle. If the traveller could not answer correctly, the sphinx killed him. The riddle asked by the sphinx was "Which animal walks on four legs in the morning, two at noon and three legs in the evening." The correct answer

The Monsters of Heracles

According to the Greeks, Heracles was the strongest man in the world. As a punishment for murder, Heracles had to fulfil 12 labours. The first was to slay a monstrous lion which could not be killed by any weapon. Heracles killed it by strangulation. Secondly, Heracles killed a hydra, a serpent with nine heads. The third task demanded the capture of a wild boar. The fourth was to capture a hind with golden horns that ran fast and tirelessly like the wind. The fifth task was to slay a flock of human-eating birds which had beaks and talons of bronze. Heracles next had to clean out the stables of Augeas, that housed thousands of cattle and had never had been cleaned, in one day. As a seventh task, Heracles captured the sacred and extremely powerful bull of Crete. Then he caught the mares of Diomedes, which ate human flesh. The ninth task was to steal the girdle of Hippolyta, Queen of the Amazons. Next, Heracles captured a herd of red cattle guarded by Geryon, a giant with three heads. The eleventh task was to fetch Cerberus, the monstrous triple-headed hound which guarded the entrance to the Underworld. Finally, the hero had to gather the sacred apples of the Hesperides watched over by an unsleeping dragon.

was finally found by a man named Oedipus who replied "A man. As a baby he crawls, as a man he walks and as an old man he uses a stick."

Further east, in modern Iraq, the civilizations of Assyria and Babylon flourished. These people believed in the existence of good and evil monsters. The wicked monsters were known as

The monsters of Greek legend were brought to the screen in the 1963 movie Jason and the Argonauts. *Top left: Poseidon, god of the sea. Top: Jason battles with living skeletons. Above: Talos, a giant bronze man.*

Half-man Half-horse

The centaurs were strange monsters. They had the bodies of horses, but the torso, head and shoulders of men. The centaurs were said to be very wise. Several gods and heroes are said to have been educated by centaurs. But centaurs were also exceptionally barbaric. Centaurs loved to drink alcohol to excess, fight and indulge in all sorts of cruelty. These strange monsters were said to live on the slopes of Mount Pindus in Greece.

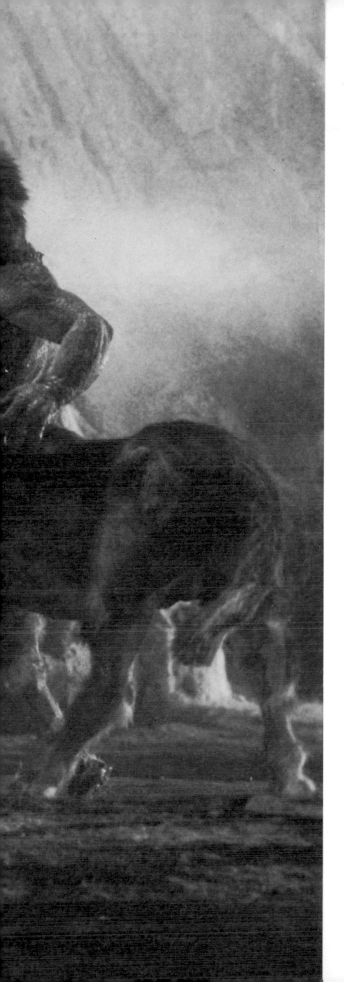

utukku and appeared in the form of hideous, half-human beasts. One particularly nasty creation had a human body, a lion's head and sharp talons on its feet. Friendly monsters were no less dramatic. One had an eagle's head while others took the form of gigantic bulls with human heads.

The greatest hero of the region was Gilgamesh, who acquired much of his fame when he slaughtered a monster named Khumbaba. This ferocious beast was three times larger than a man, his mouth was filled with sharp fangs and his hands carried great talons. The monster was so frightful that Gilgamesh only managed to overpower it with the aid of the gods.

The ancient writings of past civilizations are full of stories of fantastic monsters. Many of these beasts were depicted in art and on buildings. Through these media, the monsters are familiar even today. Films and books featuring these classical heroes and monsters are still produced for our entertainment.

The Monster of the Storm Cloud

The mighty Greek monster Chimaera is considered to be a personification of the storm cloud. The ferocious beast is described as having three heads, those of a lion, a goat and a dragon. Each head could breathe fire, the lightning of a thunder cloud.

Dragon of Babylon

On the ancient walls of Babylon are carved a number of animals, most of which represent real animals. The exception is a creature called a sirrush. This beast has a scaly body, clawed feet and a long neck. Some people have suggested that this strange creature is not fictitious. Because it is depicted alongside real animals, perhaps this monster may have actually lived at the time of the Babylonians.

The Golden Voyage of Sinbad *brought to life many mythical monsters including a centaur (half-man half-horse) and a griffin (half-eagle half-lion).*

The heir of Bamburgh approached the serpent which lived on the beach by the castle.

Dragons

Several centuries ago the people of Europe believed that enormously powerful reptilian monsters named dragons prowled the landscape. Many tales were told of these tremendously powerful monsters. They summed up all the wild, ungovernable energy of nature in a stupendous creature far more dangerous than any other known to man.

Many considered dragons to be rare, but dangerous animals were occasionally encountered, usually with fatal results. Only a very few warriors or knights could defy a dragon. Most people fled in fear from the terrible monsters which destroyed everything in their path. Most dragons were said to be natural animals, but some tales, however, indicate that at least some dragons were the result of magic and enchantment.

About the year 1270, the lord of Bamburgh Castle, Northumberland, married a second wife. The lord's son and heir was abroad at the time, but his daughter, Margaret, was at home. For some reason the new wife, who was really a witch, took a dislike to her stepdaughter. The witch transformed Margaret into a hideous serpent. The horrible creature made her home on the beach near the castle and drank the milk of seven cows daily.

Some time later, the heir of Bamburgh, whose name is said to have been either Wynd or Owain, arrived home. He was confronted by the hideous serpent on the sands and drew his sword to protect himself. The monster, however, begged Wynd to kiss her. Showing rather more nerve than most men might, Wynd kissed the hideous beast. Instantly, the beast turned

The Benevolent Dragons

In China, dragons were believed in just as firmly as in Europe. But Chinese dragons were not the ferocious killers of Europe. Instead they were friendly creatures which controlled the weather and rivers or protected the gods. The Chinese believed that there were nine types of dragon, each of which had its own powers and importance.

back into Margaret. At the same time the witch became a toad and was imprisoned under the castle, where, so the story goes, she remains to this day.

A far more traditional dragon was that encountered by the great hero Beowulf in the land of the Geats. The story of the battle is told in an ancient poem which was written about 1,200 years ago. A mighty dragon lived in a deep cavern where, many years earlier, a mighty king had been buried with a hoard of gold and weapons. The dragon lay on the mound of gold, guarding it against any intruders.

One day, however, a man stumbled upon the cave and made off with a golden cup. The dragon was enraged and began to destroy the surrounding countryside. It ate people and livestock and burned houses with its breath.

Beowulf, King of the Geats, and a few companions set out to kill the monster. When Beowulf reached the dragon's lair, the monster rushed out and fought him. Beowulf beat the monster back but then "the seething dragon attacked a second time; shimmering with fire the venomous visitor fell on his foes, the men he loathed. With waves of flame, he burnt the shield right up to its boss". In the battle which followed, Beowulf was killed but not before he mortally wounded the dragon.

The dragon encountered by Beowulf loved gold, but the other favourite possession of dragons was beautiful young women. Near the city of Kiev, in Russia, there is said to have been a dragon named Gorynych. This dragon lived on a fertile plain near the city and attacked anyone who entered the plain. The beast also flew outside its territory to raid and destroy farms. On one of these trips, the dragon carried off the daughter of the King of Kiev.

A young warrior in the city, named Dobrynja Nikitich, galloped off after the dragon. He caught up with the hideous monster in a cave, where the princess and others were held prisoner. Using a whip made from the finest silk, Dobrynja beat the dragon into submission.

Another dragon which was defeated by a rather unusual weapon was that which inhabited the lands of King Herodd of Sweden in the 9th century. The beast was causing so much damage to Sweden that Herodd offered his daughter Thora in marriage to anyone who could kill the monster. Many warriors took up the challenge, but they all failed.

Then, in the middle of winter, Ragnar of Denmark came to Sweden. He noticed that the dragon breathed poison, not fire. Ragnar made himself a suit of long, shaggy goatskin and then leapt into river. When he emerged, Ragnar was encased in wet goatskin. This froze into an extremely tough suit of icy armour. When Ragnar attacked the dragon, his icy suit protected him from the poison and he was able to kill the monster. Ever after this feat Ragnar was known as Ragnar Hairy Trousers.

One of the most famous dragons was the Lambton Worm. This ferocious beast was known as a worm because it had neither legs nor wings. The worm was caught in the River Wear, in County Durham, by the heir to Lambton. At this time the worm was only a few inches long. The heir threw the ugly creature into a well. A few years later the heir left for the Crusades.

The worm, meanwhile, had grown to a huge size. It burst out of the well and stalked the surrounding countryside searching for food. The hideous beast ate cattle, sheep and even people. After seven years, the heir returned home to find his lands devastated. He visited a local wise woman to ask her advice. The woman told him to attach spikes to his armour and fight the dragon on a rock in the river. However, the woman warned that the heir must afterwards kill the first thing he met, or his family would be cursed.

A powerful dragon breathes fire in the film Dragonslayer.

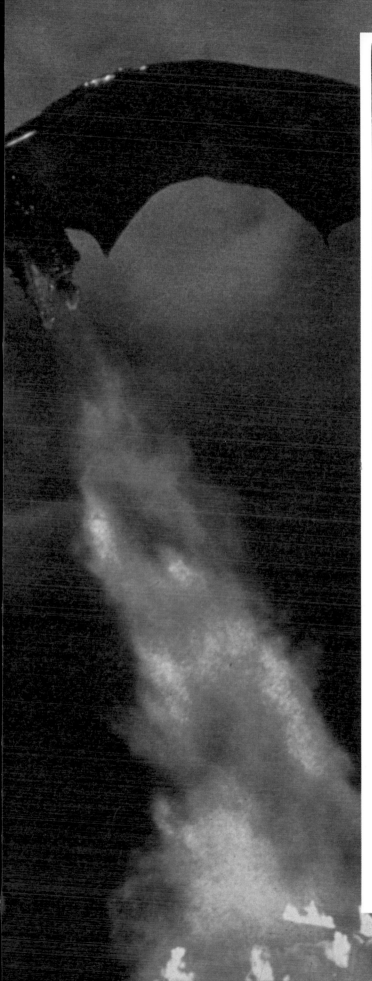

Top: a woodcut by the 16th-century German artist Albrecht Dürer which shows St George slaying a dragon.

Bottom: a 16th-century bench end in Crowcombe parish church, Somerset, shows two men tackling an unusual two-headed dragon.

Left: Ragnar attacked the hideous monster after first covering himself in frozen goatskins.

Right: an illustration from an 1875 book on the Lambton Worm.

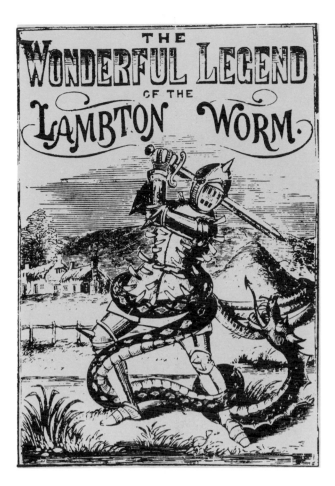

The heir took this advice and advanced against the beast. When the worm attacked, it threw itself around the heir and began to squeeze. But the spikes on the heir's armour cut the worm into pieces which fell into the river and were washed away. Before the fight, the heir had arranged for a dog to be sent to him so that he could kill it. However, in the excitement, the heir's father rushed out to greet his son. The heir could not kill his father and so brought a curse on his family so that for nine generations no lord of Lambton died a peaceful death.

The victories of Ragnar, Dobrynja and Beowulf were all exciting tales designed to be told in feasting halls and during celebrations. Though most people at the time believed dragons to be real creatures, the stories were not intended to be believed. However, some historians talked of real-life encounters with dragons. Witnesses believed that they had seen dragons and reported them to the authorities.

In 1654, for instance, a man named Paul Schumperlin was hunting in the forest near Lucerne, Switzerland, when he came across a dragon whose scales clashed together like metal. On 30 November 1222, hundreds of people watched a dragon fly over London. But the most detailed of these accounts comes from Sussex in 1614. A strange creature was seen several times in St Leonard's forest. Eyewitnesses said it was about three metres (nine feet) long and covered in scales. It was jet black, but its belly was red. Several attempts to catch the dragon were made, but they all failed.

Although no dragons are reported to have been seen for at least 250 years, they remain popular creatures in stories. Many modern writers, such as G. K. Chesterton and C. S. Lewis, still feature heroes in their books battling against hideous dragons. Dragons have even managed to maintain their place in films and on television. The film *Dragonslayer* shows that the fabulous monster is still in legend a powerful and well-known beast.

The Greatest Dragon Fighter of All

The most famous of all the legendary men said to have slain dragons is St George, the patron saint of England. St George lived during the final years of the Roman Empire. When passing the town of Silene in Egypt, he came across a beautiful young woman standing by the road, crying. St George stopped to find out what was wrong, and learnt that the girl was being fed to a dragon so that the monster would not attack the city. St George drew his sword and attacked the dragon. After killing the beast, St George persuaded the people of Silene to become Christians and to build a church on the site of his fight with the dragon. In this story the dragon is made to symbolize the evils of paganism, St George's victory representing the triumph of Christianity.

The man cut a paw from the wolf, but later discovered that it had changed into a human hand.

Werewolves

In the winter of 1558 a Frenchman asked a friend if he wanted to join in a hunting trip. The friend declined as he was waiting for an important visitor. The man set out alone to hunt in the forest of Auvergne. While in the snow-covered forest, he was attacked by a particularly ferocious wolf. Drawing his razor-sharp knife, the man fought back and sliced a paw off the wolf. He picked up the paw and placed it in his bag.

When returning home, the man stopped to see his friend and tell his story. When the paw was tumbled out of the bag, however, it had changed into a graceful human hand. The friend suddenly cried in horror. On a finger of the hand was a ring which belonged to his wife. The two

In traditional tales, the werewolf is a ferocious beast which preyed upon humans.

The Poligny Werewolves

At Poligny, France, in 1521, two men, Michel Verdun and Pierre Bourgot, confessed to being werewolves. They said that they changed form at will by undressing and rubbing their bodies with a secret ointment. The case caused a sensation throughout France and the men were executed.

men ran upstairs to find the wife bandaging a severed wrist. The woman was arrested and executed as a werewolf.

Whether the story is true or not is unknown, but it has been told many times and similar tales are related in many areas of France. For some reason that country seems to have been the centre of werewolf activities. A belief in werewolves was, however, fairly common in northern Europe. This may have been because wolves in these areas were responsible for several deaths. The ordinary villagers might assume that particularly fierce wolves were supernatural in some way.

Many cases are on record where groups of farmers, or even local officials, set out to hunt a werewolf. The descriptions of the werewolves might easily be explained as appearances of real wolves, but witnesses were convinced they had seen werewolves.

The mythical werewolf was a horrific creature and anyone who became a werewolf was to be pitied. The traditional werewolf was a person

Many werewolf attacks reported in the 18th century were probably sightings of real wolves.

who was the unwilling victim of a curse or spell. Sometimes a man was said to become a werewolf by eating a sheep which had been killed by a werewolf.

On the night of a full moon, or sometimes every night, the unfortunate man would become transformed. His skin would become incredibly hairy and his fingernails change into claws. Unable to control himself, the werewolf stalked through the night seeking a human victim to kill and eat. Some werewolves became completely transformed into wolves. Others remained basically human in shape but gained sharp wolf teeth and claws. Whichever form the werewolf took, the creature's eyes remained human. It was in this way that many otherwise normal wolves had their true supernatural identity recognized.

In some areas it was believed that a werewolf had a magical wolfskin which he put on at night to be transformed. If this wolfskin was stolen and destroyed, it was thought that the werewolf would die. Sometimes such a werewolf might be recognized in his human form if he shivered or flinched. This occurred if the wolfskin was in a cold place or if it was touched.

These traditional beliefs may have had a foundation in truth, though that is not to say that werewolves ever existed. During the Middle Ages, when werewolf tales were common, wolves roamed across much of Europe. Dark forests covered much of the land and harboured thousands of wild animals. In addition to wolves, there were bears, boars and wild cattle.

Lone travellers straying into the forests at night were in real danger of attack by a wild animal. In particularly severe winters, when food was scarce, wolves were often driven to attacking humans. Usually hunting in packs, the wolves were quite capable of tearing a man to pieces.

Once the tales of werewolves became widespread, some madmen became convinced that they were werewolves. In 1547 a group of French farmers heard a child scream and a wolf howl. The men hurried to investigate and found a young girl lying in the forest. Running off at high speed was a man. The girl had been badly bitten and remembered being dragged through the forest by a man who used his teeth and howled like a wolf.

A few weeks later the man was identified as Gilles Garnier and promptly arrested. At his trial, Garnier admitted attacking the girl. He also confessed to the murders of several other people. Garnier claimed that he changed into a wolf when carrying out these attacks. He was immediately executed for his crimes.

Thirty years later another werewolf confession occurred in France. On this occasion, however, the court realized that the confessor, whose name was Jean Grenier, was insane. No evidence was offered to indicate that he had been guilty of any crime at all. The 14-year-old boy simply seemed convinced that he was a werewolf. The court sent the boy to a monastery to be cared for, but he never recovered his sanity.

In recent years, the werewolf legend has been adopted by the cinema. The first werewolf film was produced in 1913, but it was not until more than 20 years later that the character became popular. In 1935 Universal produced *The Werewolf*, which was a modest success. In 1941, *The Wolfman* appeared starring Lon Chaney Junior and was an instant success. Chaney played the werewolf several more times and the subject became established as a favourite with film-goers. The recent productions *American Werewolf in London* and *A Company of Wolves* have brought the idea up to date in truly horrific fashion.

The Medical Werewolf

In 1963 Dr Lee Illis, a British doctor, suggested that a rare medical condition might have given rise to tales of werewolves. Dr Illis pointed out that sufferers of the hereditary disease porphyria have many symptoms previously associated with the werewolf. The sufferer's skin is intensely sensitive to sunlight, which means that he can only venture out at night. The teeth may turn red in colour and finger nails become twisted and sharp. This idea has not been accepted by many scientists, but it may have played a part in the growth of the legend.

This werewolf embodies all the evil and animal forces traditionally ascribed to such creatures. The semi-human werewolf is often featured in horror films.

The Devil King

The subcontinent of India is a vast area inhabited by millions of people. In this land beliefs in a host of supernatural and monstrous beings are common. The most ferocious of these powerful and evil monsters are generally known as demons, but there are many types of demon.

The demon which it is believed is most likely to be encountered is a rakshasa. Thousands of these creatures are said to live in a magical city which was designed by Visvakarma, the architect to the gods. In this city, Rakshasas are civilized and elegant beings which treat each other with impeccable manners. However, the Rakshasas dislike humans. Whenever they come to Earth the Rakshasas delight in causing trouble.

Though the Rakshasas can change themselves into any shape they like, they usually choose that of a hideous monster with poisonous talons and blazing eyes. They love to wander into villages and frighten the inhabitants. In stories, Rakshasas are sometimes seen as avenging spirits. They may take a dislike to a person because of some sin he has committed. In these circumstances, the rakshasas track down their quarry without mercy.

A typical characteristic of Indian gods and goddesses are their many arms, a feature used in the film The Golden Voyage of Sinbad.

The Ogres

The Indians believed in the existence of monstrous ogres with human bodies and horse's heads. These horrific creatures lived in caves close to roads and leapt out to kill passing travellers. The unlucky humans were then cooked and eaten. However, tales are told of some humans who were loved by ogres and lived with them. The children of these couples were human in form, but immensely powerful like the ogres. It was said that ogres could not cross running water, so a human could escape by leaping across a stream.

Equally dangerous are the nagas, which are believed to be snake gods. Appearing on Earth in the form of ordinary snakes, nagas will ruthlessly attack anyone who has offended them or the snakes. In southern India, it is thought wise to placate the nagas. Most farms have a small statue of a naga which is surrounded by a patch of land that no tool is allowed to touch. It is thought that by leaving a patch of ground to the snakes, the villagers will gain the favour of the nagas.

More powerful are the maruts. These crea-

tures are said to be the children of Rudra, god of animals, and Prisni, goddess of darkness. They delight in whipping up gales and strong winds which tear down trees, destroy houses and can even cause mountains to shake.

But the most dangerous of all the monsters was Hiranyakasipu, the Demon King. This enormously powerful figure was created by the gods, but soon joined the demons in spreading death and destruction. Eventually, Hiranyakasipu turned on the gods themselves. In a terrible battle, Hiranyakasipu led his demons in an attack on heaven. He succeeded in defeating Indra, the chief god, and exiling the gods from heaven.

For many years Hiranyakasipu ruled in heaven inflicting cruel tortures on any who opposed him. Eventually, the Demon King fell out with his own son and in rage kicked a pillar in his palace. The pillar split in half and the mighty hero Vishnu leapt out. After a short but terrible fight, Hiranyakasipu was torn to pieces. His demons were cast out of heaven, to continue to work mischief on Earth.

Monsters of the Dreamtime

The Aborigines of Australia believe that the entire land, together with its animals, plants and people, was created long ago during the Dreamtime. During the Dreamtime mighty monsters wandered the land and animal ancestors existed together with the first men and tribes.

Many of the monsters of the Dreamtime existed in the legends of only single tribes. But the mighty rainbow serpent was known to nearly all the Aborigines. This powerful beast was said to be responsible for creating many features of the landscape.

According to one story, the rainbow serpent fell to Earth near Cape York in southern Australia. He came across a tribe of people, but could not understand a word they said. The rainbow serpent decided to search for people he could understand. The huge snake slithered northwards through Australia, creating valleys and gorges wherever his body touched the ground.

Eventually the rainbow serpent found a tribe with whom he could speak. He taught the people many valuable skills, such as how to dance, and how to paint patterns on their bodies for celebrations. However, the multi-coloured rainbow serpent became hungry and ate two boys of the tribe. The angry tribesmen chased him to a huge mountain and attacked him. They slit open the rainbow serpent's stomach and the two boys emerged in the shape of multi-

coloured lorikeets. As the wounded monster thrashed around he smashed the mountain to pieces, creating a range of low hills. Then he dived into the sea. Similar stories are told about the rainbow serpent throughout Australia.

Another fearsome monster supposed to have lived during the Dreamtime was the giant devil dingo. This fearsome beast was shaped like a giant dog many times larger than a man. The beast was owned by Grasshopper Woman and

The Dreadful Whowie

During the Dreamtime a frightful reptilian monster called a whowie was thought to have lived in a deep cave. Each night the beast came out to hunt. It preyed upon kangaroos, wombats and humans. Eventually, the tribes of the area gathered together to kill the whowie. They lit a fire at the entrance to the cave. When the whowie emerged, it was choking from the fumes and was quickly killed by the spears and clubs of the Aborigines.

The young warrior caught a bunyip, but soon regretted his catch.

hunted people for his mistress' supper. The enormous monster was eventually killed by two cunning brothers. A medicine man then used the skin, head and kidneys of the giant devil dingo to create the first dingos. These wild dogs still roam Australia.

Another monster which features in Aboriginal legend is the bunyip. But this monster is different from other Dreamtime beasts because some people think that it may actually have existed. The Aborigines say that the bunyip lurks in rivers and lakes. It is shaped rather like a seal with a very long tail. This creature is believed to possess great magical powers and is a

dangerous creature to encounter. One young Aborigine hunter is said to have caught a bunyip. He tried to carry the beast home, but a mighty flood magically arose and forced the hunter to climb a tree. The bunyip escaped and the hunter found that he had changed into a black swan.

Such tales were told to the very first British settlers in New South Wales late in the 18th century. Stories of strange magical animals were generally disbelieved, but in 1821 the Europeans were forced to take the bunyip seriously. In that year, the famous explorer Hamilton Hume returned from an expedition to the interior. Hume reported that in the waters of Lake Bathurst, he had come across a bunyip. As the European settlers spread out across Australia more and more reports of a strange water beast were made.

In 1873, a large creature with a seal's head was spotted in a lake in Queensland. Three years later a similar beast was reported in South Australia. It is possible that the bunyip of Aborigine legend and the creatures sighted by settlers were a type of freshwater seal. Sea lions and seals have been seen many times in river estuaries. Perhaps some found their way far inland to give rise to the stories of bunyips.

The Monsters of Fire and Water

The Polynesians who live on the islands of the Pacific Ocean developed a culture ideally suited to the islands on which they lived. They harvested coconuts and bananas on the island and fished in the sea for all types of seafood. However, the islands and the surrounding ocean were not always kind to the Polynesians. Most of the islands were created by volcanoes. Violent eruptions might break out at any moment, engulfing the population in fire and ash. The seas could be whipped into towering waves by the terrible storms which swept across the ocean. Man-eating sharks and other terrifying creatures lurked beneath the waves. These constant dangers were reflected in the monsters in which the Polynesians believed.

On many islands there was said to be an all-powerful fire god, or goddess, who lived in the volcanic heart of the island. On Hawaii, the goddess was known as Pele. She controlled the mighty volcano in the centre of Hawaii Island. If any of the tribesmen offended her, perhaps by breaking a taboo, Pele poured molten lava out of the volcano to destroy everything in its path.

The inhabitants of the Fiji Islands believed in a giant which had once lived high on a mountain. This frightful figure was tremendously strong and had teeth of fire. At the time of the giant, it was believed, man did not have fire. One day a group of brave young men crept up to the mouth of the giant with bunches of coconut leaves. They held these forward until they caught fire. The young men then fled from the giant who was angry that anyone else should have fire. Eventually, the men were able to kill the giant and escaped with the fire. It is possible that this tale might refer to a volcano which became extinct, the volcano being thought of as a giant with fiery teeth.

A belief common among the islands is that each type of animal has an enormously powerful

The Polynesians are expert wood carvers and produced magnificent statues of their terrifying gods and monsters. These examples stand near Honannau on the west coast of Hawaii.

king or god. These mighty monsters roam the world looking after the members of their species. The most dangerous of these animal monsters was the great shark. This ferocious beast was the most powerful shark in the world and constantly patrolled the oceans looking for opponents to fight.

According to a story told in Fiji, the great shark was named Dakuwaqa. He loved to pick quarrels with other sea animals and force them to fight. One day he heard of a mighty monster which lived near Kadavu Island and set out to fight it. On this occasion Dakuwaqa found himself faced by a giant squid. The squid caught the great shark in its arms and defeated the aggressive monster. The squid then made Dakuwaqa promise never to attack the men of Kadavu Island. The great shark had to make the promise. Because of this promise, it was believed, sharks would not attack men who lived on Kadavu.

On the Hawaiian Islands, a similar god was said to haunt the waters of Pearl Harbor. The native islanders objected to the building of the United States naval base in Pearl Harbor as they thought that the work might anger the gods.

The temper of the gods and monsters of Polynesia was terrible and violent. Many men suffered from the consequences of angering the supernatural beings. In an environment where nature could be violent it was only natural that legendary monsters should be even more destructive.

The Giant Maui

According to most legends in the Pacific, the islands were created by a semi-divine giant who is often named Maui. The story most often told is that Maui is out fishing with his brothers when he hooks a gigantic fish. After a long struggle, the fish is hauled to the surface of the ocean, where it becomes an island. Maui is also said to have slowed the sun down, so that it stayed in the sky all day, and to have created the first dog.

PHANTOM MONSTERS

The Devil in Devon

As night drew in on Thursday 8 February 1855, snowflakes fell across southern Devon. By 11 o'clock a deep layer of crisp snow covered the land. In the early hours of the morning several dogs suddenly awoke and started to bark and growl for no apparent reason. Something strange was moving through the night.

When dawn broke the following morning, farmers and shepherds, bakers and blacksmiths got up and set out for work. Many of them stopped in amazement and surprise. Clearly defined in the snow were thousands of tiny hoofprints. The marks ran along streets and across fields, regardless of any obstructions. Where a wall stood in the path of the tracks they approached on one side and left on the other. Whatever had made the prints had simply leapt over. In some places the hoofmarks were found running across the roofs of houses and barns. Elsewhere the prints ran under bushes just 19 centimetres (eight inches) off the ground.

The early-morning risers gathered to discuss the strange tracks. The tracks were all identical. They were shaped very much like those left by a horse or donkey and about six centimetres (two and a half inches) wide. The hoofprints ran in a single line, spaced at intervals of 20 centimetres (eight inches).

But the most astounding fact was the enormous length of the line of prints. Starting at Bishopsteignton, the trail led to Teignmouth and then northwards through Dawlish to Powderham. The tracks then crossed the River Exe to Clyst St George and marched south to Lympstone, Exmouth and Littleham. In all, the prints covered more than 48 kilometres (30 miles) of the frozen landscape.

Experienced gamekeepers and farmers inspected the tracks and declared that they had never seen anything like them. At Dawlish a group of men armed themselves with shotguns and scythes and set out to hunt the mystery creature. They failed to find it.

Nobody could imagine what type of animal could possibly have made such tracks, or indeed covered such a distance in the space of a few hours. Then the suggestion was made that the hoofed prints had been made by none other than Satan himself.

That night hardly a soul left home after dark. Convinced that the Devil was in Devon, the country folk were taking no chances. Five days later more tracks appeared in Topsham and prints were reported from places as far apart as Totnes and Bicton. The vicar in one church preached a sermon in which he tried to reassure his parishioners that the prints were those of cats, but few believed him. Once again everyone remained indoors after dark. It was many days before life returned to normal in Devon. To this day nobody has been able to explain what type of creature could leap over walls, walk over houses and cover 48 kilometres (30 miles) in a single night.

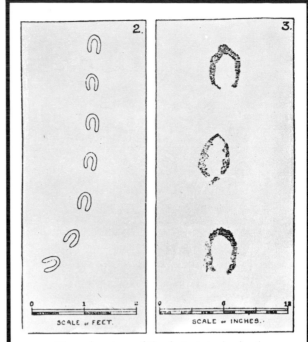

These drawings of the footprints, by local eye-witnesses, appeared in newspapers to illustrate accounts of the mysterious visitor.

Giant Dogs

Haunting the roads and paths of Britain is said to be a particularly frightening monster which takes the form of a huge black dog. Hundreds of people have come across the hound. The descriptions they give of this frightful apparition are consistent and realistic, yet the black dog has never been found. It seems to be a monster which can appear and vanish at will.

The black dog is usually seen running along the roads or sitting beside gates and bridges. It is much larger than a normal dog, some say that it is as large as a pony, and is covered in long, shaggy hair. But the most disconcerting features of the black dog are its eyes. They are as large as saucers and glow with a burning red fire. Seen on a dark country lane late at night, the black dog is a terrifying sight indeed.

In 1940 a bus driver named Nott was steering his Southern National vehicle across Exmoor near Blackmoor Gate. It was just before dawn and Mr Nott had picked up only two passengers on this isolated section of his route. Suddenly a huge dog and two sheep leapt into the road in front of the vehicle. Mr Nott slammed his brakes on, but realized he could not stop in time.

Instead of the impact he expected as he hit the animals, nothing happened. Leaping down from the cab, the bus driver looked around for the creatures. They had completely vanished. At first Mr Nott thought he had been dreaming, but both his passengers had seen the large dog and sheep as well.

More disturbing was an encounter in 1893. Two men were returning to their home in Norfolk in a cart. Suddenly they were confronted by a huge black dog standing in the middle of the road. No matter what the men did the dog would not move out of their way. Losing patience one of the men approached the dog which promptly exploded in a ball of flame. A week later the man died.

A similarly vicious apparition appeared at Blythburgh, Suffolk, on Sunday 4 August 1577. While the villagers were at prayer, the doors of the church suddenly flew open and a black dog ran in. The dark creature ran straight towards the altar. As it passed through the church, the dog touched three people who immediately dropped dead. The claw marks of this deadly visitor can still be seen on the church door.

Other encounters with black dogs are far less dangerous. About a century ago a man named Finch met a large shaggy dog on the road near Overstrand, Norfolk. Thinking that the animal was the pet of a neighbour which had bitten him earlier, Finch kicked out at it. His foot passed right through the apparition. In more recent years another man had a similar encounter with

The Phantom Dogs of Britain

Ghostly hounds have been reported from several areas of Britain and are known by a variety of names.

Shuck is the name given to the hound in East Anglia. This creature is said to prowl roads and can be dangerous if annoyed in some way.

In Lancashire the phantom dog is named Striker. Some people say that the dog appears as a warning of approaching death.

The Barguest of Yorkshire is a similar phantom to Striker.

Further north the spectral hound is named Padfoot and is said to have feet which turn backwards. This means that people who think that they are fleeing away from Padfoot are actually running towards it.

In the Hebrides a very different ghostly dog is said to haunt the countryside. Known as Lamper, this creature is pure white in colour and has no tail. It is thought to be a sign of impending death.

Lamper

Padfoot

Boggart or Barguest

Trash or Striker

Shuck or Shag

the same beast. On this occasion the man held out his walking stick to the dog, which passed straight through it.

A woman was walking home to Crosby, Lincolnshire, just before the Second World War when suddenly, a black dog with glowing eyes ran up and started to walk beside her. The woman ignored the dog, which barely seemed to notice her. A short distance further on, the woman met a group of tough-looking men. They seemed threatening and called some abusive comments at the woman. But when the men saw the monstrous creature trotting at her heels, they left the woman alone.

In 1938 a man out strolling in Norfolk saw a black dog approaching him. This man had heard tales of Shuck, as the dog is known in Norfolk. He wisely stood to one side and allowed the beast to pass him. This seems to be the safest reaction to a black dog. The majority of sightings involve people who carefully avoid annoying the dog in any way at all.

This is easy advice to follow when the dog is seen simply trotting along a road, but sometimes the black dog is said to be more positive in its actions. It is often seen guarding a particular place or route. In 1927 a man encountered a large phantom dog on a road near Ramsey, Isle of Man. The ghostly hound stood in the middle of the track and refused to move. Snarling and growling, the apparition glared steadily at the man. Realizing he could not pass the dog, the man stood quietly. After some time, the dog moved to one side and the man could continue his journey.

In the 1860s a similar guardian appeared at a gate near Melton in Norfolk. It blocked the route home of a man named Goodman Kemp.

Kemp went into a local inn and borrowed a shotgun with which to drive the dog away. However, as he approached the gate, the phantom guardian leapt forwards and bit him savagely before disappearing.

Many people have studied the phenomenon of the black dog. They have found that the descriptions of the dog given by witnesses are remarkably consistent. This indicates that whatever the black dog is, it is a real object. The behaviour of the dogs may seem to vary, but in every case the dog seems to be on guard duty of some kind. It may block a gateway or patrol a road. Some investigations have suggested that the black dogs may be guardian spirits conjured up by ancient druids or magicians. However,

nobody can be certain what the phantom creatures may really be.

It is not only in Britain that giant phantom hounds haunt the countryside. A century ago, an English traveller came across similar creatures in Russia. He was travelling across the Ural Mountains in a troika, an open sledge drawn by three horses. Suddenly a pack of wolves burst from the forest and attacked the men and horses.

Grabbing his rifle, the Englishman poured bullet after bullet into the wolf pack. Several of the savage creatures were shot, but the others closed in for the kill. Then the man heard the baying of hounds in the distance. As he desperately beat the wolves away with his rifle butt, the man saw a group of large white dogs bound into sight. As soon as the hounds came on the scene the wolves turned tail and fled.

The new arrivals made no attempt to follow the wolves, they simply trotted along in front of the troika. When the Englishman reached safety the large dogs threw back their heads and howled. Then they vanished into thin air. Only then did the man realize that he had been saved by spectral hounds.

The Great Cats

Early on 29 July 1976 two milkmen, David Crowther and David Bentley, were setting out on their milkround near Nottingham. Suddenly they found themselves staring at a sight which struck fear into them. Just 45 metres (150 feet) away was a lion. There could be no mistaking the feline stride and tawny coat of the creature. The startled milkmen fled and reported the lion to the police.

When several more reported sightings came in, the police took the lion seriously. It was assumed that the beast had escaped from a zoo or circus. However, it was later discovered that no lion was missing. The public were advised to stay indoors and armed policemen set out to hunt the lion. Within a week some 65 people believed that they had seen the "Nottingham lion", as the press dubbed the creature. Then sightings suddenly ceased and police declared that no such lion had ever existed.

The case of the "Nottingham lion" was just one incident in the long-running saga of mysterious great cats. For many years large cats have been sighted running around the British countryside. Yet all scientists agree that no such animals exist.

One of the most famous of the mystery cats was the "Surrey puma" which was seen many times during the 1960s. Possibly the first sighting was made on 16 July 1962 when Ernest Jellet visited Heathy Park Reservoir, near Farnham. He first saw a rabbit being stalked by a large animal. Suddenly the hunter pounced, but missed. The rabbit bounded towards Mr Jellet, and the larger creature followed it. As it approached, Mr Jellet had a clear view of the animal. He later described it as a small lion with large paws. Fortunately, the beast veered off before reaching Mr Jellet.

The strange cat was reported to have been seen several times over the following two years. The descriptions of the beast seemed to indicate that it was a puma. This animal is native to both North and South America, but not to Britain. It is about two metres (six feet) long and stands some 60 centimetres (two feet) tall. It is tawny in colour and preys voraciously on other mammals. The hunting activities of the "Surrey puma" began to emerge two years after the first sighting.

In August 1964 Edward Blanks, a farmer near Farnham, found one of his cattle lying in a pool of blood. It had been bitten and mauled by a large and powerful creature. The vet who attended had never seen anything like it. Mr Blanks thought that the Surrey puma was to blame. Local farmers began patrolling the woods armed with shotguns. Several thought that they saw the puma, but nobody managed to kill it. By the end of 1968 nearly 400 people had reported seeing a puma in Surrey and neighbouring counties. Then the sightings suddenly tailed off.

It is not only large cats which have been seen. In 1975 a milkman in Yorkshire turned a corner to see a bear just 20 metres (66 feet) away. In January 1980, a wild boar was seen several times in Essex. On one occasion it dug up a garden with its tusks before fleeing into nearby woods. On 16 May, a motorist in Lancashire had to brake sharply to avoid running over a two-metre (six-foot) long crocodile.

Some investigators suggest that all these sightings are simply mistakes. It is said that the reported boars, pumas and bears are really dogs or foxes seen fleetingly in unusual circumstances. However, some of the reports make it clear that the mystery animal was seen at close quarters so that there could be no mistake. Another suggestion states that the creatures have escaped from zoos. Unfortunately, such runaways are rarely reported at the same time as the mystery animals.

Perhaps the most intriguing suggestion is that the animals are neither real nor imaginary. It is thought that the creatures may be phantoms of some kind. If this were the case, the ghostly creatures would be able to appear to witnesses and then vanish before they could be caught or tracked. Some think that the beasts are ghosts of animals which once roamed Britain. Others have suggested that these creatures are demons in disguise.

But perhaps the most revealing case is that of Ted Noble of Cannich, Invernesshire. For several years in the late 1970s, Mr Noble and neighbouring farmers had been finding their sheep and cattle killed by a mystery animal. Judging by the injuries, the unknown predator was both large and powerful. A few witnesses reported glimpsing a puma in the Scottish hills. These reports were dismissed by police and scientists alike.

Ted Noble, however, believed the stories, he had seen the cat-like creature himself. He therefore laid a trap consisting of a cage which would automatically shut if a large animal entered it. Mr Noble baited the trap with meat and waited. On 29 October 1980, he went to inspect the trap. In it was a real-life puma. It was later discovered that a man had released a puma into the wild some years earlier when he was sent to jail.

The large cat-like animal bounded towards Ernest Jellet snarling savagely.

Giants

One of the few places where a giant man is said still to exist is on the slopes of Ben McDhui, a mountain in Scotland. Many climbers and locals have reported seeing a figure known as the Great Grey Man. Most have been seized with fear upon meeting the giant and some have given way to blind panic.

In 1891 Professor Norman Collie of London University climbed the 1,300-metre (4,300-foot) peak. As he descended the mountain, he passed through a bank of mist. Suddenly, Collie heard heavy footsteps following him. He peered into the mist to see what was making the noise, but was suddenly and inexplicably seized with panic. He fled down the mountain at breakneck speed.

More than ten years later the famous mountaineer Dr A. M. Kellas actually saw the giant. He caught sight of a large man on the mountain some way above him. As Kellas watched in surprise the mystery figure passed behind a three-metre (ten-feet) tall cairn. The giant was clearly taller than the cairn. In 1945 the Great Grey Man almost claimed a human life. P. A. Densham was on Ben McDhui when he heard giant, heavy footsteps. Like so many others, Densham fell into a blind panic and ran down the mountain at top speed. He only managed to stop his headlong rush a few feet short of a sheer precipice. If he had continued running he would have been killed.

The Great Grey Man is clearly a phantom, if not entirely imaginary, figure. Yet the reports and tales about him are interesting and may indicate the origin of other stories about giants.

Many countries around the world have traditions about giants. These enormous men are said to stand many feet taller than normal men and are tremendously strong. The characters of the giants vary tremendously. Some are bloodthirsty and aggressive, others are friendly and some are stupid in the extreme. The only characteristic which these many figures have in common is their enormous size.

According to the Aztecs, who ruled Mexico before the country was discovered by Europeans, the giants were all dead. It was believed that giants had lived on Earth thousands of years earlier. They had been violent and boastful creatures who spent their time building mountains and digging valleys. The gods were thought to have killed all the giants many years ago.

The Vikings also thought that the giants were enemies of the gods. The giants were said to live in Jotunheim and constantly plotted ways to enter the halls of the gods and destroy them. Many of the Viking myths are concerned with the struggle between the gods and the giants. It was believed that at some remote future date the giants would attack, aided by a host of other monsters, and overcome the gods. Known as

The Tallest Man on Earth

The tallest human measured with scientific equipment was Robert Wadlow who was born in America in 1918. Wadlow suffered from a rare disease which affected his growth rate and inflicted severe disabilities. He reached a height of 2.72 metres (8 feet 11 inches), but he died at the age of 22.

Many people have fled in panic when confronted by the Great Grey Man.

Raganarok, or the Twilight of the Gods, this day represented the end of the world to the Vikings.

Many other peoples believed that giants still existed and walked on Earth. The Ashanti tribe in Africa called giants sasabonsam. It was thought that these creatures were covered with hair and had red eyes. They were supposed to roam through the forest seizing and eating humans.

Similarly vicious giants were the wendigoes believed to exist by several Indian tribes of North America. These mythical creatures were thought to walk over lakes and through forests. Whenever they caught a human, the wendigoes would swallow him whole.

Other cultures told stories about heroes who slew mighty giants to prove their valour. One of the most famous of these tales is contained in the Bible. About 1400 BC, Israel was at war with the Philistines. The armies of the two countries came to battle but, before fighting started, a

giant strode out from the ranks of the Philistine army to challenge any Israelite to single combat. The giant was said to be 2.9 metres (9 feet 6 inches) tall and his name was Goliath of Gath.

Not a single Israelite stirred because they were so frightened of the giant. Finally, a young shepherd boy, named David, stepped forward. Though the giant was armed with a sword and shield, David carried only the sling he used to chase wolves from his flocks. However, the boy felled the giant with a single stone. Having thus proved his valour and worth, David went on to become King of Israel.

In Ireland, a race of mythical giants was thought to live in the Atlantic Ocean. Known as Fomorians, the giants were able to create storms, gales and fogs and were greatly feared by sailors and fishermen. The Irish also believed in giants which lived on land. According to one story the son of the King of Ireland became involved in a game of cards with a giant. The boy won and gained a large area of land. During a second game he won a herd of cattle, but the boy lost the third game in which the stake had been his own head. Only by magical means and with the help of the giant's daughter was the boy able to keep his head.

In England, giants were firmly believed to exist. It was said that during the 11th century a son named Tom Hickathrift was born to a farmer in Cambridgeshire. As the boy grew up he became a powerful giant, but he was lazy and simple. It is said that in the course of his life, Tom became involved in many escapades through his laziness and stupidity, but he always managed to get the better of his enemies by his superior strength.

Giants have also been connected with the origins of various objects. The Wrekin Hill, near Shrewsbury, is said to be a pile of earth carried to the site by a Welsh giant who was determined to bury Shrewsbury. The giant was dissuaded from this when he asked a cobbler the distance to the town. The cobbler realized the wicked intention of the giant so he told the giant that it was so far that he had worn out a sackful of shoes on the journey. The cobbler then produced a sack of old shoes to prove his tale. The giant dumped his spadeful of earth and went home.

At Cheselbourne in Dorset is a large stone said to be the tomb of a giant. Several prehistoric stone circles are said to be giants turned to stone for dancing on a Sunday, or some similar offence. Others are explained away as the chairs or beds of giants. Clearly these giants are nothing more than creatures of myth and legend. But there is some evidence which suggests that giants may be more than imaginary monsters.

On several occasions, the bones of enormously tall men are said to have been found. In 1705 a group of Spanish peasants claimed to have accidentally dug up a skeleton which measured some seven metres (22 feet). More than a century later explorers in Alaska said they came across three-metre (nine-foot) long skeletons. In the Philippines local villagers claimed to have found a five-metre (16-foot) skeleton just after the Second World War. None of these alleged discoveries has ever been proved to be genuine.

The angry giant was tricked by a clever cobbler from Shrewsbury.

The Giant in the Turf

On a hillside above the Dorset village of Cerne Abbas can be seen a remarkable figure cut into the turf. The chalk which is revealed shows white against the green grass and can be seen from a distance of several miles. The figure is that of a giant 55 metres (180 feet) in height who is walking across the hillside brandishing a giant club. A similar giant is to be found at Wilmington in Sussex.

Unidentified lights were photographed as they swept over Salem Air Base, Massachusetts. Some people think they are only reflections.

The Aliens

On 24 June 1947 American businessman Kenneth Arnold climbed into his light aircraft and took off to fly over the Cascade Mountains of Washington State to Yakima. He had no reason to suspect that this flight would be anything other than routine. In fact Arnold was about to open a whole new chapter on strange and monstrous creatures.

As he flew Arnold noticed nine strange aircraft in the distance. They had no wings but were flying at a startling speed as they skipped between the mountain peaks. Trying to describe the strange undulating flight path of the objects,

Arnold said that "They flew like a saucer would if you skipped it across the water." The public and press became fascinated by Arnold's "flying saucers". The speed of the saucers was far greater than any known aircraft. They were a genuine puzzle.

Soon other reports of strange aircraft began to be made. The sightings became known as UFOs, Unidentified Flying Objects. One of the most spectacular sightings came in 1965 in Amesbury, Massachusetts. Norman Muscarello was walking home late at night from a friend's house when he noticed a bright light to one side of the road. As the startled Muscarello stared in astonishment, the lights came closer and more

A mysterious line of unknown aircraft that was photographed over Montreal, Canada in August 1973.

distinct. He found himself staring at an object some 25 metres (78 feet) in diameter which had a row of gleaming red lights on its underside. The object swept past at high speed.

Thoroughly frightened, Muscarello waved down a passing car and insisted on being taken to a police station. There he told his story. Later, Muscarello showed a policeman the site of his sighting. The spectacular UFO came back into view, hovered for a while and then flew off.

Reports such as this puzzled both scientists and the public. At first nobody could imagine what the UFOs were. They seemed to perform manoeuvres which were utterly impossible. They flew at speeds which no man-made aircraft had ever reached and changed direction with such suddenness that they should be crush-

ed. Some suggested that the craft might be secret weapons of the United States Air Force, or of a foreign power. But when UFOs were reported from other countries these ideas were discarded.

In 1950 a book entitled *The Flying Saucers are Real* appeared. It was written by Donald Keyhoe, who had been studying UFOs. In the book Keyhoe advanced a theory which people had been talking about for some time. He claimed that UFOs were space ships from civilizations on other planets.

In fact, Keyhoe had little evidence for his idea.

It simply appeared that any aircraft of such astounding capabilities as the UFOs must come from another civilization. However, soon startling new evidence appeared which seemed to support the idea of alien life forms. The aliens themselves began to be seen.

One of the most famous of these sightings occurred on 24 April 1964 when a policeman named Lonnie Zamora was driving his patrol car near Socorro, New Mexico. He suddenly noticed a large flame to one side of road. Fearing an explosion or fire of some kind, Zamora drove off the road to investigate. The policeman saw an oval-shaped object standing on the desert some 140 metres (450 feet) away. Beside the gleaming oval stood two small figures. Zamora thought that they were about 1.2 metres (four feet) tall.

Climbing from his car, Zamora moved forward to investigate. The figures scrambled into the oval object which then took off with a loud roar and flew towards the horizon. Investigators found marks in the soil where the object had rested. These indicated that it had weighed about a ton.

On the same day as Zamora's encounter a farmer in New York State claimed he met aliens who were greatly interested in plants and

Norman Muscarello fled in panic until he waved down a passing car and asked to be taken to a police station.

Russell Long is holding a mysterious disc which fell from the sky to land in his Hollywood home in California, in July, 1947. Mr Long believed that the curious object may have come from outer space.

fertilizer, collecting samples of both. Also fascinated by plants were the little men which a French farmer named Maurice Masse is said to have encountered in his fields near Valensole on 1 July 1965.

Masse started work in his lavender fields soon after dawn. When he saw what he thought were young boys stealing his flowers, Masse decided to creep up on them. He had got within five metres (15 feet) of the figures when he realized they were not boys at all. The figures had large round heads and were dressed in tight green clothes.

Suddenly one of the figures spun round and pointed an instrument at Masse. The farmer felt himself to be paralyzed. After gathering lavender, the unwelcome visitors climbed into a gleaming oval object which flew off. Masse remained paralyzed for some time, but eventually managed to run off for help.

The strange men reported by Masse and Zamora seemed to be disinterested in humans. However there is increasing evidence that at least some "aliens" are dangerous and aggressive. On 10 December 1954 two Venezuelan boys, Lorenzo Flores and Jesus Gomez, were returning from hunting rabbits when they saw what they thought was a crashed car in some bushes. The two boys went to investigate, only to find that the metallic object was a gleaming disc hovering above the ground.

Suddenly four small hairy figures leapt out of the disc and ran towards the boys. The little figures attacked the boys with long sharp talons which gashed the boys badly. Gomez was wrestled to the ground and the aggressive strangers began dragging him towards their craft. Armed only with an unloaded shotgun, Flores flung himself at the beings and managed to rescue his friend. The boys then fled to a police station, which sent them to hospital to have their injuries treated.

Similarly aggressive were the little beings which were reported by a Kentucky family on 21 August 1955. One member of the family watched a UFO land in the woods. Soon afterwards the farm dogs began barking. Two of the men went outside to see what was causing the commotion. They were startled to see,

advancing towards the house, a small figure with arms raised above its head. The figure was just over a metre (four feet) tall and had long pointed ears and claw-like hands. The men barely hesitated. One grabbed a shotgun and another a rifle. Both shot the little man at point blank range, knocking it off its feet.

The men rushed indoors, to find other little men trying to climb in through windows. Once again the guns roared and the strange figures retreated. For the next three hours the intruders tried to get into the house and grab the humans. The bullets fired at them seemed to take no effect. Finally the terrified family dashed to their car and fled to the nearest town.

These frightening reports indicate that the beings associated with UFOs can be far from friendly, and even dangerous. However, it is not clear what the figures might be. Some people believe that they are intelligent life forms from other planets. These aliens are thought to be visiting Earth either to make contact with humans or simply to explore the planet. However, many investigators do not think this is a likely explanation. No habitable planet is close enough to provide a base for such visitors and it is difficult to imagine any civilization using the wide variety of craft described by witnesses. Another theory suggests that the UFOs are time travel machines from the distant future of Earth.

It has even been suggested that UFOs do not exist at all. Many scientists think that the witnesses reporting UFOs are misidentifying objects such as bright stars or conventional aircraft. While this may be true of many sightings, some cannot possibly be fitted into this scheme.

More imaginative researchers have suggested that UFOs belong to another dimension which exists in parallel with our own universe. The ability of UFOs to appear and vanish at will, and the startling manoeuvres they follow seem to indicate that they are not machines obeying the laws of physics as we understand them. Perhaps they are more similar to ghosts and phantoms than to spacecraft.

The encounter of January 1988 in Sidona, western Australia, gave rise to a revealing comment by the hapless policeman investigat-

The most expensive and exciting science fiction film of its time was the 1953 War of the Worlds, *from which these scenes are taken.*

ing the report. A family was driving along a road when a glowing object flew down and landed on their car. The UFO then lifted the car into the air and dumped it some distance further on. Four small dents were later found in the car roof. When interviewed by radio reporters, the policeman declared "Something out there sure scared these people and we would like to get to the bottom of it." So would everyone interested in UFOs.

The Flying Monsters

Many people have reported seeing winged monsters swooping and soaring through the air. These creatures range from unidentifiable beasts in remote regions of the world to phantom animals terrorizing densely populated areas.

A game warden in Africa during the 1930s heard many native tales of a gigantic bat-like creature which was said to live in what is now Zambia. Known as the kongamato, this beast has been reported by many explorers and tribesmen. Most accounts agree that it has a wingspan of about four metres (12 feet) and wings of skin. A few witnesses have identified the kongamato with pictures of pterodactyls, which lived at the same time as the dinosaurs.

The mention of ancient flying reptiles surviving to the present day echoes the terrifying experience of two sisters in Texas in 1976. Walking beside a pond near Brownsville, the girls were startled to see a huge creature wheeling around in the sky above them. When the monster dived down towards them, the sisters fled. Later the girls searched through an encyclopaedia to try to identify their mysterious attacker. When they came to a picture of a *Pteranodon*, a type of pterodactyl, they both recognized it instantly. Several similar reports have been made in Texas over the past 50 years, but no satisfactory explanation of what is seen has been advanced.

A spate of strange sightings occurred in Cornwall during the 1970s. Named the Owlman, this beast had red eyes and was the same size as a man. One feature of the Owlman was that many sightings took place near churches, which suggests a link with a beast which terrorized Renwick, Cumbria, in 1845. Described as a man-sized bat of extreme ugliness, it first appeared when the church was being renovated and has been seen several times since.

These flying apparitions seem very real to witnesses, yet they are never caught. It is impossible to know whether the beasts are real or phantoms, or just the figments of over-imaginative minds.

The Owlman was sighted by many people in Cornwall.

MAN-MADE MONSTERS

Monsters in Books

Monsters have been favourite subjects in fiction for centuries. The power and ferocity of such beasts seems to have exercized a strong hold on the imaginations of those who created stories and poems. Ugly or ferocious monsters could be used by the writer to punish a wicked character. In other circumstances a hero could prove his true worth by slaying a creature of phenomenal strength.

The ancient Greeks and Romans told stories of hideous mythical creatures which wrought havoc amongst mankind. These beasts were sent by the gods who had been angered by the behaviour of humans or fellow gods. The monsters in these stories are usually killed by a semi-divine hero.

During the Dark Ages which followed the collapse of Roman civilization many poems and sagas were composed which featured dragons and other monsters. *Beowulf*, one of the oldest complete poems in English, tells the story of a man-eating water monster. These creatures were depicted as natural monsters, rather than curses sent by gods.

However, it was during the last century, when most people learnt to read, that fictional monsters became truly popular. One of the first was a werewolf named Wagner. In 1857, the story of this beast was unfolded in a series of 77 chapters. Each chapter was published seperately and cost one penny. Because of their cost and subject matter, such publications became known as "penny dreadfuls". The low cost of the parts ensured that they could be afforded by almost everybody. The tale of Wagner was written by a man named George Reynolds, who produced several similar works.

A very different type of monster also made its first popular appearance in the penny dreadfuls.

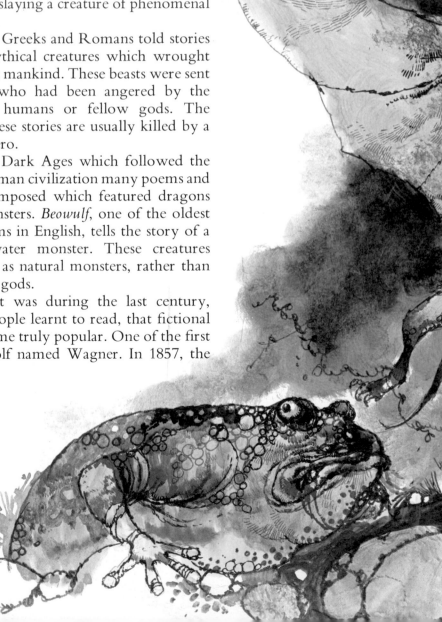

In 1847 the first chapter of *Varney the Vampire* was published and the tale eventually ran to a total of 868 pages sold in weekly sections. In that same year a boy was born in Dublin who, as Bram Stoker, would make vampires and other monsters famous with his writing.

Bram Stoker (1847–1912) wrote *Dracula*, his great vampire novel, in 1897. The story concerns a young English estate agent, named Jonathan Harker, who travels to Transylvania to sell property to a nobleman. Harker is horrified to learn that his customer is a vampire and the novel describes the struggle between the monster and Harker.

Stoker is less well known for his other works, such as the short stories *The Squaw* and *The Judge's House* and the novel *The Lair of the White Worm*. This novel was Stoker's last work and in some ways his strangest. It tells the story of Adam Salton, a rich Australian who comes to live in his family home in Derbyshire.

There he meets a beautiful young woman named Lady Arabella March, who strikes him as odd on their first meeting. Snakes seem to vanish whenever Lady Arabella is near and other animals behave oddly. Salton's pet mongoose viciously attacks the woman who responds with equal violence and kills the little animal.

After many adventures, Salton is forced to realize that Lady Arabella is the human manifestation of a large and hideous white worm which lurks in a deep well. In this novel Bram Stoker is drawing on traditional beliefs about dragons and monstrous worms. However, unlike the gallant mediaeval dragon slayers, Salton does not tackle the beast with sword and shield. He throws dynamite into the well and blows the creature to pieces.

The explorers in the novel The Lost World *came across aggressive pterodactyls and a huge, warty toad.*

In the last quarter of the 19th century a new writer emerged who wrote many novels and short stories which featured monsters. The man was a doctor by the name of Arthur Conan Doyle (1859–1930) and his work was so highly esteemed that he was later knighted.

One of the most exciting monster tales he produced was *The Lost World*. Published in 1912, this book pretended to tell the adventures of a group of explorers who had travelled up the Amazon. Early editions of the book even included a photograph which claimed to show the explorers themselves. In fact, the whole story was fiction and the photograph showed imposters.

The tale, however, is a masterpiece of monster fiction. It opens by describing the journey of the group as they penetrate deeper into the rainforest. When the expedition approaches a mysterious plateau, they sight a huge pterodactyl flying through the air. They manage to climb the steep cliffs surrounding the plateau

No sooner had he stepped ashore than Gulliver was attacked by the hideous Yahoos.

and find themselves confronted by a succession of prehistoric monsters. The climax of the tale comes when the explorers meet a race of primitive humans.

Ten years before completing *The Lost World* Arthur Conan Doyle produced a novel in which a fake monster plays a dominant role. While visiting Dartmoor, Doyle had heard tales of a phantom black dog which prowled the bleak moor. He wove this idea into his novel *The Hound of the Baskervilles*. The plot concerns a Dartmoor family haunted by a large phantom hound. After the death of the head of the family has been blamed on the dog, the famous detective Sherlock Holmes is called in to investigate.

In this tale, however, there is no monster at all. The spectral dog is a clever fake produced by a neighbour who hopes to gain from the deaths of the Baskerville family.

Writing at much the same time as Doyle was H. G. Wells (1866–1946) who saw himself as much as a campaigner as a writer. Many of his finest works were intended as comments upon society. Wells had a vivid imagination which he

used to invent many monsters. In 1901 his *The First Men on the Moon* followed the adventures of a group of astronauts who arrived on the Moon to discover it populated by a race of incredible creatures.

More famous were the space monsters which Wells invented for *The War of the Worlds*. The book opens as a strange object falls from space in to a wood in Surrey. From the device emerges a weird alien machine which destroys everyone who attempts to approach it. Soon other aliens arrive with deadly weapons and march out across the land in an attempt to conquer the world. Earthly guns and explosives seem to have no effect and it seems as if the world is doomed. Finally, however, the aliens die because they have no immunity to Earth diseases.

Wells also produced the chilling tale of *The Island of Dr Moreau* in 1896. The book is written in the first person and opens as the narrator is persuaded to accompany two other men to a remote island.

The Japanese Monster

One of the oldest Japanese poems tells the story of a brave young warrior named Susa No who set out to kill a ferocious eight-headed monster which was threatening to devour a beautiful princess. By using his cunning, Susa No was able to get the beast drunk on saki. The intoxicated monster then stood little chance against the flashing sword of Susa No. When the monster was killed, the poem continues, the warrior married the princess and later inherited the kingdom.

One of these men seems odd. He is very hairy and walks clumsily. On the island the narrator discovers the horrible truth behind the strange man. He is a result of the terrible experiments of Dr Moreau. This scientist has hidden himself away on the island to try to transform animals into men. Many half-human creatures inhabit the island, together with other cross-bred creatures.

Gulliver was rescued by the horses.

The Nonsense Monsters

In the last half of the 19th century a series of nonsense poems were produced by Lewis Carroll, author of *Alice in Wonderland*. Some of these contained fantastic creatures of which perhaps the three most famous are introduced in the opening lines of *Jabberwocky*.

'Twas brillig, and the slithy toves
Did gyre and gimble in the wabe;
All mimsy were the borogroves,
And the mome raths outgabe.

"Beware the Jabberwock, my son!
The jaws that bite, the claws that catch!
Beware the Jubjub bird, and shun
The frumious Bandersnatch!"

Though at first glance it may seem that the creatures are the monsters of the tale, the book gradually reveals that it is Dr Moreau who is the evil one. His experiments have inflicted suffering on his victims. As animals the creatures were well suited to their environment, but now that they are half-human they are not adapted to either a life in civilization or in the wild. Eventually, the creatures revert to their animal state and take a hideous revenge upon Dr Moreau.

Another writer who successfully used the

In a particularly horrific scene in the book The Rats, *published in 1974, a man is eaten alive by a horde of rats.*

The Imagination of J.R.R. Tolkien

When producing his great cycle of books *The Lord of the Rings*, the British writer J.R.R. Tolkien used many features of folklore. Fairies, wizards and goblins appear in various guises within the stories.

In *The Hobbit* a huge mound of treasure, which rightly belongs to the dwarves, is guarded by a hideous dragon named Smaug. This dragon is only defeated after a great fight, and the use of cunning.

theme of half-human monsters to criticize society was Jonathan Swift (1667–1745). As a journalist, clergyman and politician Swift dominated much of society during the early 18th century. However, it is as a satirist that he is usually remembered today.

In 1726 Swift produced his masterpiece *Travels into Several Remote Nations of the World, by Lemuel Gulliver*, now more commonly known as *Gulliver's Travels*. Swift himself said that he wrote the book "to vex the world rather than divert it", an aim which he achieved brilliantly. The early chapters, concerning Gulliver's visits to Lilliput, the land of little men, and Brobdingnag, the home of giants, are both amusing and biting comments on society of the time.

The later chapters, however, are more disturbing. Gulliver finds himself abandoned by a mutinous crew on a strange coast. Moving inland, Gulliver came face to face with a monstrous figure. Covered with thick fur on its head, chest and back, the creature caused Gulliver to remark "Upon the whole, I never beheld in all my travels so disagreeable an animal."

The beast blocked Gulliver's path and refused to let him pass. Gulliver drew his sword and struck the animal with the flat of the blade. The creature uttered a loud shriek and instantly, Gulliver found himself set upon by about 40 of the ugly beasts.

Gulliver was rescued from his predicament when a group of horses approached and frightened the monsters away. Gulliver was startled to discover that the horses were in fact highly intelligent and were talking to each other. They called the horrible beasts Yahoos. Gulliver ran forwards and tried to explain that he was an Englishman, but the horses thought he was a Yahoo. Only then did Gulliver realize that the ugly Yahoos are actually very human in appearance.

Slowly Gulliver learnt the language of the horses, who called themselves the Houyhnhnms. They turned out to be gentle and civilized creatures who despised the barbarous Yahoos. In telling the story, Swift points out the savage and baser instincts of humans through the

For a moment he struggled frantically, then heard a hoarse cry, and wrenched his head up to see a dark shape speeding across the plateau from the opposite edge. It was Coburn. Twisting in the remorseless grip of the two with whom he battled, he had a flashing glimpse of Coburn racing toward the machine, and then he uttered a cry of agony. From one of the hovering cones above, a shaft of the light-ray had flashed down and it struck Coburn squarely. A moment he was visible, aureoled in a halo of blinding light. . . .

An illustration from the magazine Amazing Stories *of 1927, showing a scene from H.G. Wells' story* The First Men in the Moon.

actions of the Yahoos. On the other hand he treats the animals in a much kindlier way, emphasizing the gentleness and innocence of their nature.

Alongside human-beasts, another fictional theme much used by writers to point out deficiencies in society is that of ordinary animals turning against humanity. Usually the creatures are driven to such behaviour by the attitudes of man.

According to a well-known German tale from the Middle Ages the wicked Bishop Hatto stored large amounts of grain while the neighbouring peasants were dying of starvation during a famine. Determined to stop the constant complaints, the bishop invited all the peasants to a great banquet. Eagerly, the starving folk poured into Hatto's hall. But when everyone was inside, Hatto barred the doors and set fire to the building. As the wretched peasants died, Hatto remarked callously "That should stop the mice from squealing."

However, when neighbouring lords heard of

Hatto's cruelty they set out to punish him. The bishop fled to an island in the Rhine and locked himself inside a strong tower. When he turned from the door, Bishop Hatto was horrified to find that the building was swarming with mice which, like the peasants, were starving in the famine. The creatures leapt on the wicked bishop and ate him. The Mouse Tower, where Hatto is said to have met his grisly death, can still be seen at the town of Bingen.

A similar attack by rodents featured in the book *The Rats* which was published in 1974. In the story a man sleeping rough in the East End of London awakes to find himself being bitten by a very large rat. More of the horrible creatures join the attack and the man is quickly killed and eaten. In the course of the novel, written by James Herbert, it becomes clear that the vicious rats are not ordinary rodents, but some kind of mutants being directed by an intelligent power. The climax of the novel comes when the master

"This apparatus seemed only reasonably large and near to us, and then I saw how exceedingly little the Selenites upon it seemed, and realized the full immensity of cavern and machine. It was stupendous!"

Another illustration from the magazine Amazing Stories, *which was staggeringly successful during the 1920s in America.*

A scene from the classic film The Birds, *in which flocks of birds make deadly attacks on humans.*

rat, a snow-white creature with two heads, is tracked to its lair.

James Herbert went on to write several more horror books after the success of *The Rats*. In some the monsters are terrible manifestations of real animals, but in others they are subtler creatures which are only glimpsed.

The theme of revolting nature has been exploited in several horror novels and films. Crabs, spiders, frogs and worms have all played their part in attacking humanity, but perhaps the finest of these tales was *The Birds*. The short story by Daphne du Maurier focused upon a small Cornish community which suddenly finds itself under attack by vast flocks of birds. *The Birds* was filmed in 1963 by the master director Alfred Hitchcock. The combination of chilling plot and magnificent filming make the story terrifying however much it is enjoyed.

Monsters and the terror they inspire remain as popular as ever, though their form may change with the times.

The Marvel Monsters

The writers of the Marvel comics have invented a wide range of terrifying monsters which feature in their works. One of these is Dr Octopus, a scientist who has become hideously mutated by a nuclear accident. Armed with long mechanical arms, this evil genius hopes to take over the world. A similarly changed individual is the Lizard, a doctor who accidentally turned himself into a giant lizard. More wicked is Bi Beast, a fantastic, two-headed monster which ferociously guards his home. An enemy which features in many adventures is Annihilus, the king of the Negative Zone, another dimension existing beside our own Universe. Determined to spread his power into our dimension, Annihilus comes into constant conflict with the superheroes of the Marvel comics.

Monsters of the Screen

The visual impact of monstrous creatures make them ideal subjects for films and television. A huge ugly head thrusting forwards from the screen is guaranteed to make an audience jump with fright. This fact was recognized in the earliest days of cinema and has been exploited ever since. Film makers looking for suitable monsters had a wide variety from which to choose, and some created their own beasts.

The beasts which are found in myths and folklore have been used in films for years. The audience can immediately recognize a werewolf, dragon or vampire, so the film does not need to waste time explaining the monster to the public. It can leap straight into the story. Horror movies, in particular, have exploited the possibilities of traditional monsters.

In 1914 the old Jewish fable of the golem, an artificial man of clay brought to life by a magician, was made into a silent epic by the German director Paul Wegener. Other masters of the silent films produced movies about vampires and monstrous beasts of every description.

It was with the coming of sound, however, that the traditional monster came to the screen in a big way. Werewolves first appeared in *Werewolf of London* in 1935, but did not become a great success until Lon Chaney Junior took up the role. In *The Wolf Man* (1941), the werewolf became firmly established as a film monster. He has continued to appear in various guises, perhaps most spectacularly in *American Werewolf in London* which told the story of two young Americans who fall victim to a werewolf in Yorkshire. One dies but the other survives to become the beast of the film title.

It was the perfection of stop-action techniques which brought the mythical monster to the screen. This method involves using a model monster which is filmed one frame at a time and moved slightly between each shot. When these frames are superimposed on those of an actor a realistic monster is created.

In *The Seventh Voyage of Sinbad* (1958) this technique was brought close to perfection by Ray Harryhausan who called this method dyna-

These hideous monsters from the film An American Werewolf in London *show the skill of the make-up artist.*

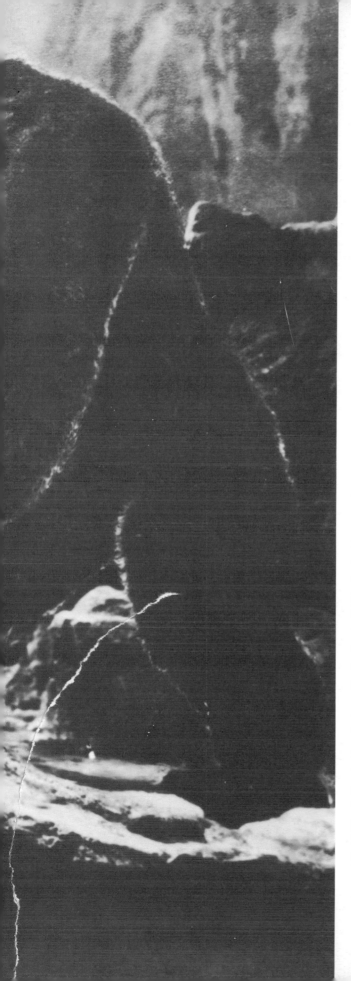

mation. This, and subsequent Sinbad movies, featured a realistic snakewoman, a many-armed goddess, a dragon and several giants, all of which battled realistically with a human Sinbad. Harryhausen recreated his success in the 1963 movie *Jason and the Argonauts* which centred on one of the great legends of ancient Greece; Jason's search to find the golden fleece. During his voyage, Jason and his men come across such mythological monsters as the harpies (supernatural winged beings that carried off people), tritons (sea gods who were half-man and half-fish) and sword-wielding skeletons.

The ability to animate realistic models and mix them with live action was also used by directors who wanted to feature long-extinct monsters in their movies. In *One Million Years BC* a highly dramatic, if historically inaccurate, encounter between cavemen and dinosaurs was recreated with realistic effect. A rather more accurate portrayal of prehistoric life came with *Quest for Fire* in 1981. This movie abandoned the dynamation technique. Instead, elephants were dressed in red fur coats to simulate woolly mammoths with a fair degree of success.

Animated models were also useful for portraying monsters which burst their way into the modern world. In the 1969 picture *Valley of the Gwangi*, a group of cowboys find a secret canyon in the American West in which dinosaurs and other prehistoric animals have survived. Hoping to make a fortune, the adventurers drag a ferocious *Allosaurus* back to civilization. The beast escapes and leaves a trail of destruction behind it, until it is cornered and destroyed.

The theme of a gigantic monster on the loose was explored in the famous *King Kong* of 1933. This movie has become a classic of monster movies, and deservedly so. More than $500,000 were spent on the special effects alone, a stupendous sum for the time. A variety of techniques were employed to produce the very believable giant ape. Back projection, in which actors are filmed against a screen on which a film is being projected, played its part. Other new techniques

Models and other special effects were first used extensively in King Kong *in 1933.*

used included overprinting one film onto an-other and shooting a scene through a sheet of glass on which a scene had been painted. These created the illusion of large structures and giant animals. No less than 27 models were used in the film. There were tiny Kongs for distance shots, larger models for close ups and a giant arm for the scenes where Kong holds the heroine Fay Wray in his hand.

Kong's battles with prehistoric monsters on the island where he lived and his climb up the Empire State Building were believably filmed. The mixture of special effects techniques used in *King Kong* is particularly successful as it does not

Top left: the marshmallow man from Ghostbusters. *Bottom left: the massive man-eating shark from* Jaws. *Above: The evil gremlins from the film of that name. Right: a scene from* The Dark Crystal. *Bottom right: R2D2 from* The Return of the Jedi.

overshadow the actors and the plot.

Another monster which was little more than a gigantic example of a real creature was the great white shark of *Jaws* which appeared in 1975. The film was a staggering success, easily justifying the estimated $8 million which it cost to make. The film opens with a terrifying shark attack on a lone swimmer at night, which immediately sets the scene for horror and violence.

As the attacks continue, a local oceanographer realizes that a giant shark is frequenting the bathing beaches. Local authorities are unwilling to publicize the threat because they fear this would destroy their tourist trade. Eventually, however, they are forced to take the threat seriously and the action of the film shifts to the open sea.

A professional shark hunter named Quint, the oceanographer and a local policeman set out to kill the great white. In an horrific climax, the shark kills Quint and destroys his boat before it is finally killed. The mixing of shots of real sharks with scenes involving a giant model was expertly done and made the film a masterpiece both of horror and monster movies.

Jaws was made by a relatively-unknown director named Steven Spielberg. The stunning effects of *Jaws* made Spielberg a prestige figure

who could command high fees, and he has produced a string of popular movies. One of these was *Gremlins*, which featured little creatures very different from the gremlins of RAF tradition.

In the film, the gremlins first appear as a cuddly little creature bought as a pet by an American businessman in the Far East. The man from whom the creature is bought warns the businessman not to feed it after midnight. When he returns home the businessman gives the animal to his son. However, the creature suddenly multiplies and the furry animals manage to get hold of some food at the prohibited hour and undergo a frightening metamorphosis. It becomes an evil, ugly creature intent upon causing as much damage and destruction as possible. The beast rapidly multiplies to produce a small army of similar animals which take over a small American town, killing and destroying as they go. Only the prompt action of the son manages to avert a major disaster.

In *Close Encounters of the Third Kind* Spielberg tackled the subject of UFOs. This film follows the adventures of a man who sights a number of UFOs and is profoundly affected by the encounter. The special effects in the film are truly stunning. Glowing objects sweep through the sky and along highways with startling clarity. The highway chase scene is particularly well filmed.

The plot of the earlier sections of the film is

Two very different film monsters. ET (main picture) was a friendly alien, while the creature from the Black Lagoon (inset) was aggressive.

The Creature from the Black Lagoon

Produced in 1954, the movie *The Creature from the Black Lagoon* has become a classic monster movie. In addition to its chilling title, the film is typical of many monster movies produced at this time. A hideous being, played rather obviously by a man in a costume, rises from a lagoon in the Amazon delta to attack humans, in particular a pretty woman played by Julie Adams.

---

based upon some of the better-documented sightings of UFOs. The behaviour of the strange objects is as fantastic and purposeless as most reports indicate. These traits are skillfully woven into a story which is unique to the film. The witnesses to UFO activity become obsessed with Devil's Tower, a hill in the USA. They try to reach the mountain, but most are stopped by the government. In the stunning finale to the film, the UFOs land at Devil's Tower to reveal themselves as the spacecraft of aliens friendly to mankind, a conclusion not entirely in accord with evidence about real UFOs.

Even further removed from reality is the charming fairytale of a movie *ET*, also directed by Steven Spielberg. This particular film recounts the adventures of a small extraterrestial, the E.T. of the title, which is stranded on Earth and desperately wants to return home. The little creature is cared for by a boy with a BMX bicycle with whom he shares many adventures before the film's conclusion.

Also sharing in the fashion for alien monsters was the box-office smash *Star Wars*. Not only is there a lumbering, hairy giant named Chewbacca which helps the hero of the movie, but a collection of other beasts taking a more minor role. In a particularly visual scene, a bar room is crowded with many wildly differing aliens, all of which are intent on their own business and ignore the action of the film.

Not all modern films are concerned with monsters from outer space. The comedy thriller *Ghostbusters* concerns itself with phantoms and poltergeists of various kinds. These entities dominate the scene for much of the film, but the climax of the movie comes when a pagan deity reappears in New York. This god calls into existence a terrible destroyer which, due to a mistake by one of the heroes, materializes as a giant marshmallow man. This must be one of the most unusual monsters ever to come to the screen. With a face of harmless innocence and a cuddly body, the towering giant stomps through New York destroying vehicles and causing panic wherever he goes. No doubt film makers will continue to produce monsters, but few will be more innocent in appearance than the giant marshmallow man in *Ghostbusters*.

Acknowledgements

Ardea: Peter Green 13 inset; Associated Newspapers Group Ltd 17 top left, 17 top centre, 17 top right; Bruce Coleman Limited: Alain Compost 32; Mary Evans Picture Library 8, 26, 78, 100, 101; Fortean Picture Library 10, 13, 21 top, 21 bottom right, 43 top right, 43 bottom left, 43 bottom right, 57, 73 top inset, 73 bottom inset, 89, Loren Coleman 45, René Dahinden 24 top, 41 bottom, 44, M.P. Meaney 24 bottom; Photographie Giraudon 48–49; Ronald Grant 105 top; Hamlyn Group Picture Library 55; Robert Harding Picture Library 53 (from the Douce Collection, The Bodleian Library); Pat Hodgson Library 49; The Kobal Collection 14–15, 41 top, 50, 72–73, 82–83, 105 bottom left, 105 bottom right, 115, 116–117, 120 top, 120 bottom, 121 top left, 121 top right, 121 bottom, 134; Lord Hunt 36; Mansell Collection 51, 65, 78, 111; Mansell Collection – BBC 19; The National Film Archive 134 inset; Trustees of the National Gallery 52; Gary Parfitt 68–69, 116 top, 116 bottom, 118–119; Popperfoto 39 top, 103; Royal Geographical Society 38, 39 bottom, 40, 43 top left; Syndication International 18, 21 bottom left.

Cover illustration
Peter Dennis

*Numbers in **bold** refer to captions*